Jonathan Edwards

Inscriptions
on the Grave Stones
in the Grave Yards of Northampton
[Massachusetts]

and of

Other Towns in the Valley of the Connecticut

as

Springfield, Amherst, Hadley
Hatfield, Deerfield, &c.

with Brief Annals of Northampton

Transcribed by
Thomas Bridgman

HERITAGE BOOKS
2007

HERITAGE BOOKS
AN IMPRINT OF HERITAGE BOOKS, INC.

Books, CDs, and more—Worldwide

For our listing of thousands of titles see our website
at
www.HeritageBooks.com

A Facsimile Reprint
Published 2007 by
HERITAGE BOOKS, INC.
Publishing Division
65 East Main Street
Westminster, Maryland 21157-5026

Copyright © 1850 Thomas Bridgman

Originally published
Hopkins, Bridgman & Co.
Northampton, Massachusetts
1850

— Publisher's Notice —
In reprints such as this, it is often not possible to remove blemishes from the original. We feel the contents of this book warrant its reissue despite these blemishes and hope you will agree and read it with pleasure.

International Standard Book Number: 978-0-7884-0590-7

PREFACE.

Northampton, Dec. 1, 1850.

THE object of the Compiler in the work he has undertaken is to preserve in a durable form some most interesting but rapidly perishing memorials of our Puritan ancestors. He has taken much pains to trace and to transcribe the inscriptions correctly.

T. B.

From the first settlement of Northampton in 1654, to 1661, a period of 7 years, there were 10 deaths. The place of burial was Meeting House Hill. The Town voted that after Oct. of that year no more burials should be on that spot, and the present yard was selected for that purpose. The first person buried therein was Henry Curtis, the only person who died that year; but no monument designates the place of his interment, nor that of others, for many years. Among this number was Rowland Stebbins, ancestor of all of the name now in America, who died Dec. 14, 1671, aged 77, to commemorate whose death a Granite *Cenotaph* has been erected, which will be noticed in the Sequel of Monumental descriptions.

RECOMMENDATIONS.

Greenfield, July 31, 1850.

The subscriber cheerfully recommends to his friends and acquaintance, the proposed compilation of the inscriptions, epitaphs, &c. in the Northampton and Springfield Burying Grounds, by Mr. Thomas Bridgman. Such a work, he believes, will be highly interesting, not only to the inhabitants of those towns and vicinity, but throughout the Commonwealth. In the list will be found the names of some of the most distinguished men of our country, and the record of the same, as taken from the stone that marked their final resting place will be esteemed of no ordinary value by the patriot as well as the relative and friend.

T. STRONG,
Rector of St James Church, Greenfield.

We also concur in the above, as it will aid many having a desire to trace their ancestry.

DANIEL STEBBINS.
GEORGE E. DAY, *Pastor Edwards' Church, Northampton.*
RUFUS ELLIS, *Pastor 2d Congregational Church,* "
HENRY BURROUGHS, *Rector St. Johns' Church,* "
D. M. CRANE, *Pastor Baptist Church,* "
THOMAS MARCY, *Pastor M. E. Church,* "
E. Y. SWIFT, *Pastor 1st Congregational Church,* "

Hadley, Aug. 7, 1850.

I approve of the design of Mr. Bridgman's Book, and trust it will secure the favor and patronage of many in this section of the country.

JOHN WOODBRIDGE, D. D.
Pastor First Church in Hadley.

Northampton, Aug. 16, 1850.

The subscriber recommends the publication of this book.

W. ALLEN, D. D.
Late President of Bowdoin College.

I like the form of Mr. Bridgman's work. I should think such a work would have a rather large sale.

EDWARD HITCHCOCK, D. D., LL. D.
President of Amherst College.

BRIEF ANNALS

OF

NORTHAMPTON.

NORTHAMPTON, at the foot of Mount Holyoke, is generally regarded as the most beautiful village in the valley of the Connecticut, perhaps in New England.

1653. Certain Inhabitants of Springfield, 24 in number, petitioned the General Court for liberty to make a settlement at *Nonatuck*, about 15 miles up the river, representing that the place was suitable to erect a town for the furtherance of the public weal and propagation of the Gospel, and obtained permission. In the records of the company the name is written variously, *Nonatuck, Nalwottoge*, and *Norwottuck*. The accent being on the last syllable, the words, in the indistinct enunciation of the Indians, will appear to be the same. Thus on the records, Pewongenug is also written Pewongenuck. Rev. John Eliot uses the 'Indian word Noautuck, as meaning, in the midst of the River.' By its windings the meadows of Northampton, Hadley, and Hatfield are in the midst of the River.

1653, Sep. 24. John Pynchon bought *Nonatuck* of the Indians; a large tract on the west side of the Connecticut River, including Northampton and other towns. The Sachems, or Chiefs, who signed the deed, were *Chickwallopp*, or *Wawhillowa, Nenessehalant, Nassicohee*, and *Paquahalant*.

The witnesses were Elizur Holyoke, Henry Burt, Thomas Cooper, and Thomas Stebbins. The payment was 100 fathom of wampum, 10 coats, the plowing of 16 acres, and a few small presents.

As he made the purchase in behalf of the petitioners, he assigned the land to them in 1662. In November certain regulations were made concerning those, who should go up in the next spring to settle at 'Nallwottoge.'

1*

1654, May 9. Two settlements being proposed, Pynchon, Holyoke, and Samuel Chapin, by appointment of the General Court, laid out the bounds of the first settlement at Nonatuck, extending from the little meadow (Hatfield) to the Great Falls, and 9 miles back, and west from the river. Mount Holyoke is probably named after Mr. Elizur Holyoke. The town is now commenced and this may be regarded as the date of the first settlement.

Of the 24 petitioners, only 7 were among the settlers,—namely, Robert Bartlett, William Clark, Edward Elmer, John Gilbert, William Janes, William Miller, and Thomas Root. Others came from Windsor, Hartford, and Dorchester. The name of Northampton was adopted. Nov. 18. The first marriage, David Burt and Mary Holton.

1655. May 2. The first birth; Ebenezer, son of Joseph and Mary Parsons. May 30, James Bridgman born.

1656, Jan. 14. The first death, James, son of James and Sarah Bridgman. In this year there were nine births. Among the settlers were Joseph Parsons, Isaac Sheldon, and Samuel Allen.

1657, June 25. A town meeting was held, a grant of land was made to Joseph Parsons, and Samuel Allen. It was agreed to procure a minister. Measures taken to protect the Indians from the evils of intoxicating drinks.

July 30. Lampancho, sachem, sold to the town Pewongenug for 30 shillings ; this was included in the former purchase.

1658. The first meeting to raise money to defray town expenses, amounting to 130 dollars, 110 of which were for ministerial services. It was agreed to allow Rev. Mr. Mather, as a salary, about 350 dollars a year. He began to preach here in July.

Oct. 17. The title to *Capawonk*, the little meadow in Hatfield, relinquished on condition of a settlement by the next May on both sides of the river,—in Hatfield and Hadley.

1661, June 18. The church was gathered ; and the first minister, Eleazer Mather, son of Rev. Richard Mather of Dorchester, was ordained. The seven ' pillars' of the church, the seven men, first organized as a church,—were David Wilton, William Clark, John Strong, Henry Cunliffe, Henry Woodward, Thomas Root, and Thomas Hanchet ; John Strong, was the ancestor of the late Governor Strong ; Henry Woodward was the ancestor of the late Dr. Samuel B. Woodward. John Stebbins and others appointed to build a meeting house, 42 feet square, at an expense not exceeding 150 pounds. The first militia company organized. The burials, after October, no longer on meeting house hill, but in the present cemetery. Woratuck, or Hadley was settled, long called New Town. The word may be the same as Norwattuck.

1662. The following are the names of the inhabitants, eight years after the settlement :—Geo. Alexander, Samuel Allen, Alex. Alvord, Edward Baker, Robert Bartlett, Thomas Bascom, James

Bridgman, John Broughton, David Burt, Joshua Carter, William and Nathaniel Clark, Aaron Cook, Henry Cunliff, widow Curtiss, Nathaniel Dickinson, Alex. Edwards, Zachery Field, Thomas Ford, Rich. Goodman, David and Thomas Hanchet, William and John Hannum, Robert Hayward, William Holton, William and John Hulbert, Jona. Hunt, Ralph Hutchinson, John Ingersoll, William Janes, John King, Geo. Langton, Walter Lee, William and Thomas Lewis, Rich. John, and Robert Lyman, Thomas Mason, Eleazer Mather, John Miller, Joseph Parsons, Nathaniel Phelps, Medad Pomeroy, Thomas and John Root, Thomas Salmon, Isaac Sheldon, William Smead, Christopher Smith, John Stebbins, John and Thomas Strong, and J. Strong, jun. Geo. Sumner, Mrs. Williams, Ensign Wilton, Thomas Woodford, Samuel Wright, and S. W. jun., and Henry Woodward. Such is the connexion of families, that Rev. W. Allen of N. is a descendant not only of Samuel Allen; but, also by his father, of Thomas Ford, John Strong, Isaac Sheldon, Joseph Parsons, and Thomas Woodford; and, by his mother, of John Strong, and Henry Woodward.

May 7. This town, Springfield, and Hadley constituted the county of Hampshire.

1663. The first school was organized.

1664. Measures to restrain the youth from disorderly behavior on the Sabbath.

1665. Deacon Samuel Wright died, from whom descended the late Governor Silas Wright of New York.

1667. A court House erected.

1669, July 24. Rev. E. Mather died; during his ministry there were 71 church members. Measures to prevent the Indians from doing damage on the Sabbath, and to counteract the evil example of their drinking and profanity.

1672, Sept. 11. Rev. Solomon Stoddard was ordained. He was minister 56 years. His descendants remain in N.

1675. King Philip's war began. Robert Bartlett, Thomas Holton, Mary Earle, Samuel Mason, Praisever Turner, and 9 others were killed by the Indians. Hadley was attacked, but the people under Gen. Goffe repulsed the enemy.

1676, May 19. In the 'Fall fight,' so called, near Deerfield, of the 38, who were killed, were Capt. Wm. Turner, and 14 others from Northampton; among whom were John Miller, Thomas Roberts, Joseph Fowler, William Howard, and John Foster. Perhaps some were soldiers, not settlers. In a few days afterwards, Hatfield was attacked and 12 houses and barns burnt; but 25 bold young men from Hadley charged the large body of the enemy and put them to flight. It was voted to accept a garrison of 50 men. The meeting house and several houses were palisaded. Joseph Hawley invited to teach a school.

1677. The number of church members was 76.

1679. Up to this year more than 500 church members had been admitted.
1683. A great revival of religion ; also in 1690, and 1712.
1684. Died Nehemiah Allen, the ancestor of Gen. Ethan Allen.
1689. The town palisaded from half a mile to a mile square.
1692. A fine of 12 pence imposed for every non-attendance upon a town meeting.
1694. A salary of £40 to the schoolmaster for the next twenty years.
1695. Mr. Stoddard relinquished all debt of the town to him.
1697. An order for a foot bridge over Mill River to South-st.
1699. The town ordered, that no more candle wood should be collected for use within 7 miles of the Meeting House, on forfeiture of the same. Elder John Strong died, aged 92 : his descendants numerous.
1700. Pine trees not to be boxed for turpentine within 3 miles.
1703. Jan. 17. Col. John Pynchon died. A sermon by Mr. Stoddard on his death was published.
1704. Capt. John Taylor, and 10 of the name of Janes, and 10 others killed by the Indians at Paskhommuck, at the foot of Mount Tom. Killed at Deerfield Mrs. Williams, daughter of the Rev. E. Mather.
1706. The number of church members was 96.
1708. Joseph and Samuel Parsons killed by the Indians.
1711. Samuel Strong jr. also killed by them.
1712. A Grammar school ordered to be supported for 20 years : it has never been discontinued. To this time there was only a bridle path to 'the Bay,' or to Boston.
1713. A water privilege at the foot of Mt. Tom to Benj. Stebbins, on condition that for 4 years he sell boards at 20 shillings a thousand feet.
1715. An alms house erected on meeting house hill.
1720. Elder Preserved Clap died.
1724. Nathaniel Edwards 2d, was killed by the Indians at the corn mill.
1726. The town granted Round Hill to Col. J. Stoddard for 40 pounds.
1727, Feb. 15. Rev. Jonathan Edwards, was ordained as colleague in the ministry with his grandfather, Mr. Stoddard.
1729, Feb. 16. Rev. Mr. Stoddard died : during his ministry, the admissions to the church 630. Of the sermons of Rev. Mr. Williams of Hatfield, and of Mr. Edwards on his death the town requested copies for the press.
1735. A revival of religion ; 200 converts in 6 months, 10 of them about 90 years of age.
1736. The number of church members was 620.
1737. The new meeting house, 70 by 46 feet, built on meeting

house hill, near the old one, with a steeple : it lasted till 1812. The men were seated at the south end, the women on the north side, the young men alone in the gallery, the children in front of the pews.

1740. Mr. Whitefield preached at Northampton ; great attention to religion : revivals in 150 congregations.

1746. From 1729 to this year, Mr. Edwards being the minister, the admissions into the church were 495.

1747, Oct. 9. Rev. David Brainerd, missionary, died at the house of Mr. Edwards, aged 29. Jerusha Edwards, betrothed to him, died a few months afterwards, aged 17, and was buried at his side.

August. Elisha Clark killed by the Indians. He was the last of between 50 and 60 deaths by Indians, as states on the records of the town.

1748. Col. John Stoddard, a man of great influence in public affairs, died in Boston. The number of polls, and estates about 350.

1750, June 22. Mr. Edwards was dismissed : in August he removed his family to Stockbridge. He died at Princeton, March 22, 1758, aged 55. For more than 23 years was he in the ministry in Northampton. The cause of his removal was his maintenance of the principle, that the Lord's supper is designed for those, who in the judgment of charity are true christians ; in opposition to Mr. Stoddard's views, who regarded it as a converting ordinance. The church now adopts the principle, for which they rejected him.

1753, Dec. 5. Rev. John Hooker was ordained ; he died of the small pox Feb. 6, 1777. Southampton was incorporated as a separate district ; Rev. Jonathan Judd, had been the minister of this 2d precinct since 1743 : he died 1803.

1755, August 17. Capt. Hawley, Lt. Pomeroy and Thomas Wait killed at lake George.

1756, August 26. Died Abigail Alvord, aged 102 ; her name before marriage was Phelps.

1760. A letter of Joseph Hawley was published, in which he humbly acknowledged his sin in the efforts, which he made for the removal of Mr. Edwards ; and he also expressed his belief, that 'the town and church' were lying under ' great guilt in the sight of God,' for which they should pray for forgiveness, and their repentance for which, now that Mr. Edwards was dead, should be manifested by their vindicating his character and honoring his memory.

1767, Oct. 6. Elisha Alvord gave a deed of a lot in the center of Northampton, ' To the Inhabitants of the *County* of *Hampshire*,' in consideration of 130 pounds paid by Ebenezer Hunt, Timothy Dwight, Jr., Seth Pomeroy, Caleb Strong, Solomon Stoddard, Samuel Clark, Ephraim Wright, William Lyman, Seth Lyman, John King, Samuel Parsons, Jonathan Allen, Selah Wright, Joseph Allen, Joseph Cook, Joseph Lyman, Benj. Sheldon, Jr., Quartus Pomeroy, Elisha Lyman, Gideon Clark, John Hodge, Hezekiah Russell, Thomas Bridgman, Elijah Southwell, Asahel Clapp, Abner Barnard, Daniel Hitchcock, Wm. Mather, Levi Shepherd, Eliphaz Strong, Seth Clapp, Elnathan Wright, Joseph Parsons, Haines Kingsley, Timothy Parsons, Anson and Enos Kingsley, Asa Wright, Josiah Parsons, Jr., Titus King, Oliver Lyman, Elihu Lyman, Elkanah Burt, Ebenezer Clapp, Elihu Clark, Pliny Pomeroy, Abijah Wait, John Parsons, Jr. Simeon and Jos. Clapp, Joseph Hutchins, Lemuel Lyman, David Lyman, Elias Lyman, Jr. and Asahel Danks of Northampton, and Sam'l Fairfield of Hatfield.

The land, thus purchased by the principal inhabitants of Northampton, was by them given to the County, expressly for but two objects, 'for the purpose of a Green, or Common, and for erecting a Court House, or Court Houses thereon.'

Very improperly, by some mistake, the County Court was induced to license in 1816 the Selectmen to erect a Town Hall on this Lot, close to the Court House, to the great injury of the beauty of its situation,—to the inconvenience of the inhabitants of the County, who frequent the Courts, and to the destruction in part of the Small Public Green in the very center of the Town.

It is understood, that the County Commissioners have full power to *revoke* the License, which was given in disregard of the provisions of the Alvord Deed, and to order the removal of the old Town Building from the County Lot, and to restore the site of it to the use of the County as 'a green or common.' Respectable memorialists of various Towns in the County have already presented the subject to their consideration. We may expect, that as intelligent and worthy men, the express guardians of the rights of the County, they will do their duty.—In the mean while, the Town has an opportunity voluntarily to pursue the path of justice and honor, and to restore the land to the sole uses, for which the former Fathers of the Town, the ancestors of most of the present inhabitants, purchased it and gave it 'to the inhabitants of the County.' The Town having erected a new and elegant Town Hall on a different lot, has no longer an occasion for the old building, as a Town Hall, and can use it only to rent or to save a little expense ; and if, by possibility, they could now legally hold it, yet they could not in justice to the County and with a sentiment of honor to the memory of their Fathers.—As we have to do at present with the grave yard, we will say, it would be strange, if any worthy man in Northampton, out of economy, should rob the grave yard of his Father's Monument to make it a stepping stone to the door of his house.

1771, April 30. Died Col. Tim. Dwight, grandfather of President Dwight.

ANNALS OF NORTHAMPTON.

1775. Dr. Wm. Mather, and Rev. J. Hunt of Boston died.
1778, June 6. Rev. Solomon Williams was ordained : he was in the ministry 56 years. Westhampton was incorporated as a town, including a tract 4 miles wide from the west part of Northampton : Rev. Enoch Hale, was ordained the minister the next year.
1785. Easthampton was incorporated as a district ; and as a town in 1809. Rev. Payson Williston, yet living, was ordained in July, 1787.
1788, March 10. Joseph Hawley, Esq. died, a grandson of Rev. Mr. Stoddard. He was a distinguished lawyer, and statesman.
1790. The population was 1628 ; in 1800, it was 2100 ; in 1810, it was 2631 ; in 1850, it was 5309.
1801. March, a great flood.
1805, Jan. 5. Phebe, wife of Noah Parsons, died ; she was the daughter of Wm. Bartlett, and at the age of four or five years was a convert, as was stated by Mr. Edwards in one of his books.
1806. Sarah, relict of S. Baker, died, aged ninety-eight.
1809. Widow Margaret Rust, died, aged ninety-five.
1812. Oct. 28. New Meeting House dedicated : the old house stood a few feet south-easterly. Widow Hannah Wright died, aged 98.
1819. Nov. 7. Caleb Strong died, aged 74. He was Governor from 1800 to 1807, and from 1812 to 1815. His ancestors were Elder John, Ebenezer, Jonathan and Caleb.
1820. Dr. Ebenezer Hunt died.
1822. The Court House burnt. It was built in 1813.
1823. Present Court House built.
1825. The Unitarian church formed. The pastors have been Rev. Edward B. Hall, ordained Aug. 16, 1826, till Dec. 6, 1829 ; Rev. Oliver Stearns, Nov. 9, 1831 to March 31, 1839 ; Rev. John S. Dwight, May 20, 1840 to 1841 ; and Rev. Rufus Ellis, the present minister, June 5, 1843.
1826. The admission into the Church, 117. Episcopal Church organized. The ministers have been Rev. G. Griswold, 1826, Rev. Jos. Muenscher, 1828 to 1831, Rev. W. Chaderton,, 1835, Rev. D. Devens, 1838, Rev. Orange Clark, D. D. 1841, Rev. Henry Burroughs, 1843 to the present time.
1829. Solomon Stoddard died, aged 94 : High Sheriff before the revolution.
1831. The admission into the Church, 164.
1832. The number of Church members was 728. The "Edwards Church," so called, being a Colony from the Old Church, was formed ; the Ministers of which have been Rev. Dr. John Todd, now of Pittsfield, and Rev. John Mitchell. Rev. Geo. E. Day, the present Minister, ordained Jan. 12, 1848.
1834. Rev. Solomon Williams died, aged 82. His Colleagues,

who are now living, though not in Northampton, were Rev. Dr. Mark Tucker, from March 10, 1824, to Aug. 16, 1827; Rev. Dr. I. S. Spencer, from Sept. 11, 1828, to March 12, 1832; and Rev. Dr. Joseph Penney, from June 5, 1833, to Nov. 23, 1835.

1837. Nov. 7. Rev. Charles Wiley was ordained, and dismissed Feb. 26, 1845. Dr. W. is now one of the Ministers of Utica.

1843. April 15-18. A great flood of the Connecticut. The number of members in the first church was 515.

1845. Connecticut River Rail Road from Springfield to Northampton was opened.

Nov. 19. Rev. E. Y. Swift ordained over the first church.

1846. Nov. 24. Rail Road to Greenfield opened. Rev. D. M. Crane took the charge of the Baptist Church.

1847. Round Hill Water Cure opened by Dr. Denniston; now under Dr. Hall. Rev. Dr. C. J. Tenney, formerly Minister of Newport, and of Wethersfield, died, aged 67. Joseph Lyman, formerly High Sheriff, died, aged 80. He gave the town the lot for the Boy's High School. Dr. Charles L. Segur died, aged 85.

1848. Dr. Denniston's new Water Cure Establishment opened.

June. Nine children of Benjamin Tappan, who died in 1831, aged 83, met from different States at Northampton — Benjamin, John, Arthur, Charles, Lewis, &c., at the average age of 68 years: all living in 1850, at the average of more than 70—an unequalled family longevity. John Tappan gave his father's estate for a female school.

1849. Dr. Munde's Water Cure. New Town Hall erected.

1850. Dr. Samuel B. Woodward died.

June 22. A cenotaph erected by Dr. Daniel Stebbins to Jonathan Edwards, 100 years after his dismission.

Methodist Meeting House built. Rev. Tho. Marcy pastor.

Nov. 20. Philip Princeley, an Irishman, 104 years old, retaining his sight, and hearing, and mental powers, and able to do a little work in spinning.

1850. From 1654 to 1850, the whole number of Births, 3911; Marriages, 1538; Deaths, 4830. The record is imperfect.

EPITAPHS.

> "Go where the ancient pathway guides,
> See where our sires laid down
> Their smiling babes, their cherished brides,
> The patriarchs of the town;
> Hast thou a tear for buried love?
> A sigh for transient power?
> All that a century left above,
> Go, read it in an hour."--HOLMES.

NORTHAMPTON.

The oldest Monument in the *Old Burying Ground*, is about one rod west of a pine tree on the hill, at the east end of the yard. It faces the east, is much defaced by time, and all that is legible are the following letters and figures.

```
         CAP
  E       G       8y
  D       M        8
       1683 or 1685.
```

It is supposed to have been, Cap. E. Gray, (or Elisha Graves), Died May 8, 1683 or 1685.

THOMAS
HOSMER AGED
83 yERS HE
DyED APRILL 12
1687

LIEVTEN
WILLIAM CLARKE
AGED 81
yEARS D.E^d
IVLy 19 1690

EPITAPHS.

C. H.
AGED 17 yEA
RS WHO DyED IN
IVLy ANO 1690

T. H

LIVtENAN
iOHN LIMAN
AGED 66 yER
DyED AvGst
the 20th 1690

HERE LyETH THE BODy
OF MAIOR Aaron Cook
AGED Abovt 80 yEARS
WHO DyED SEP the V.
ANNODOM 1690

This stone is on the east side of the old burying yard, and is about two feet square.

IOSEPH
LIMAN SoN
oF JOHN LIMAN
AGED 21 yEARS
DyE^d FEBRY 18
1691

M^r   HENRY
  bVRT   DyEd
SEP^t   26   1735
  AGED 75 yEAR

ETITAPHS. 15

DEACON
IONAthAN
HUNT AGED 54
yEARS HE DyED
SEPt 29 1691

HER
LyES—INTERD
THE—BoDy oF MOS
ES—LyMON WHo
DyE^D THE 28 oF FEB
RUARY IN THE 38
yEAR oF HIS AGE
IN THE yEAR
1701

EXPERANC
PARSONS DA
VGHTER oF EB &
HA WRIGHT WH
DyED IVNE 5
IN ye 20 ye oF HER AGE
1715

Here lies intered
The Body of
BENJAMEN KING,
of Northampton,
who dyed IANVRy
20 1718 in the
44th year of his
AGE

WAIT ye WIFE
oF MoSES———PERSONS
DyE^d oN SEP^t ye 9
1731 AGE^d 20
yEAR

HERE LyETH the
Body of MR John
Hunt Who DyED
April yᵉ 15ᵗʰ A D
1713 in the
45ᵗʰ year of
His Age

HERE LyETH
THE BODy oF
SAMVEˡ BARTLETT
who DyED oN FEBVARy
26 IN THE 73 yEAR oF HIS
AGE. ANNODOMINI 1711

HERE LyETH
THE Body
oF
SARAH BARTLETT
who dyed IANVRY 17
IN 67 yEAR oF HER
AGE ANODOMINI 1716

HERE LyETH THE
Body oF DECON
MEDAD pVMRY
WHO DyED DECEMBER 30
1716 IN THE 79 yEAR
oF HIS AGE

KATRON
SHELDoɴ DyEᵈ
oN NOVR yᵉ 9
1727 AGEᵈ 16
yEAR

SIMEON JUDD

Noᴛᴇ.—On the east side, near the new Town tomb.

EPITAPHS.

Here lieth Intered
The Body of Deacon
SAMUEL ALLIN, Who
Died March yᵉ 29th,
1739, In the 64th
year of his age.

Father of Joseph A. and Grandfather of Rev. Thomas A. of Pittsfield, Mass., Rev. Solomon A. of Northampton, Mass., and Rev. Moses A. of Georgia, who died at Savannah in the Revolutionary war.

IN MEMORy oF
MRs MARY yᵉ
WIFE oF MR Ebenezᵉʳ Wright
who died the
15 of April
1748 aged 65
yEARS

NOTE.—A dark colored stone about 20 inches high, on the east front of the Old Burying Ground.

HERE LIES yᵉ Body
of MR NATH.ⁿ Curtis
who died August
18 1749 * * * * *
yEAR oF * * * * *

IN MEMORY of
MR AMOS LOO
mis who DIED
SEPᵗ 10th 1756
in the 25 yEAR
of his AGE

2*

HERE Lyes THE Body
of MERCY CLARK The
wife of Joseph Clark,
the Daughter of
Ebenezer & Mary
Wright Jun. who Dyed
February y° 14
1735 in the 22
year of her Age.

Note.—The first person that died in Northampton, west precinct.

Here lieth the Body
of M\rs Rachel
y° wife of M\r Gi
d * * ark who
Died Sep. 7 A D
1*49 in y° 26
year of her Age.

Here lie y° Body of
Mr. Thomas Judd
Who Died Decem\br
y° 31 Anno Dom
1749 In y° 59
yEAR of his age.

In Memory of
Lievt John
Miller who
Died April 30
1758 Aged
58 years.

Ensign
NOAH
ST * * *

Note.—This stone is broken, and lies on the ground near the east front of the yard.

EPITAPHS.

This in Memory
of Mrs. HANNAH
Relick of Lieut.
John Miller who
Died Nov 16th
1762 In the 62
year of her
Age.

Here is buried y^e
Body of JOSEPH
BASCOM son of
Mr. Joseph Bascom,
who died Feb^r
15 ANNO DOM
1749-50 aged
12 years.

In Memory of
Mr Ebenezer Wait
Died.—
October 4 1755
in ye 44th year
of his age.

In Memory of
Capt PRESERVED
CLAP who died
October 11 1757^8
in ye 83^d year
of his age.

NATHANIE
ALEXANDER
Dy^{ed} oN NOVIEM^r
ye 10 1725 AGED
49 yEAR
IOH^n HIS SON^s S

EPITAPHS.

In Memory of
Mrs Mehetabel y^e
widow of Capt
Preserved Clap,
who died Oct^r
1, 1767 in ye 85
year of her age.

Here lies the
Rev. John Hooker
Who died of the small pox, 6 February, 1777, in the 49 year of his ministry. In him an excellent and cultivated genius, graceful elocution, engaging manners, and the temper of the gospel united to form an able and faithful minister, and to render him exemplary and beloved in all the relations of life. The affectionate people of his charge, in remembrance of his many amiable and christian virtues, erected this monument to his memory.

Here lyes
Intered the
body of Eunice
Lyman daughter to
Benjamin and Thank
ful Lyman of North
hampton who dyed
Iune 1, 1720 in the
fourteen year of her
age.

M. L

The above is on a stone about 18 inches square, the letters 3½ inches.

AbIGAll
WIFE oF NATH^L PHELPS
DyED oN IaNR.
yE 1723.^{4} AGED
*27 yERS.

EPITAPHS.

HERE LyEth
y^e BODY oF
AbIGAll y^e
WIFE SAMV^l
FAIREFIELD W^{Ho}
DyE^d oN IEN^r
XIII 1726 AGE^d
27 yEAR AND
PRVDENCE FAIR
FIELD D$_y$ED on
IEN^r XX 1726
AT 13 DAYS
OLD.

ABRAHAM MILLER
dyed on Feb^r
the 7 1727
aged 58 years.

Sarah y^e wife of
Cap. IOHN PERSONS
dye^d on April y^e 15 1728
age 69 years.

CAP^t
IOHN
PERSONS, DyE^d
oN APR^l y^e 19
ANNO^d 1728
AG^d 79 yEAR.

Here lyeth
the body of
PELATIAH HOLBROO
K who died on the
12 Nouember
17-3. 8. in the 22
year of his age.

EbEN^r
STRONG
DyED oN y^e
9 oF IVNE
1725 AGED
17 yEARS.

Here lies
Intered
the body of BENI
AMIN KING of
Northampton who
died Ianuary 20th
1718 in the 44th year
of his age.

Hannah
wife of
ELIA^m KING
dye^d on OcR
10 (1723) age^d
27 yEAR.

EbENR
bVRT   DyE
IN   IVNE   1728
AT 5   yEAR   oL^d.

M^R
EbEN^R STRONG
DyE^D oN NoR y^E 12
1729   AGE^d 59
yEA^r.

AARON STR
ONG   DyE^d AVG^t 2
1732 AGE^d 12 yEAR
EbEN^r SON.

EPITAPHS.

Here is intered
The Body of the
Rev. Mr. SOLOMON STODDARD A M
Sometime fellow of Harvard College, Pastor of ye Church in Northampton, N. E. for near 60 years, who departed this Life 11 February 1729 and in the 86 year of his age; A Man of God, an able Minister of the New Testament, singularly qualified for that sacred Office and faithful therein; A light to the Churches in general, a peculiar blessing to this; Eminent for the holiness of his life, as remarkable for his peace at death.

SAMVELL
WRIGHT DyE^d oN
OC^{tr} ye 7 1732
AGE^d 49 yEAR
SAM^l SoN.

SARAH
WIFE of M^r SAM^l
WRIGHT DyE^d
APR^l ye 4 173,^{3}2
AGE^d 76 yEAR.

M^r
SAM^l
CLARK DyE^d
oN AVGS^t y^e
5 1729 AGE^d
NER 76 yEAR
WHO bVRY^d 4 SON^s AND
5 DAVGHT,^{rs}.

HERE LIETH THE
BoDy oF LIEU,T
IOHN PARSONS
who died Sept
14 1746 in the
73 yEAR oF HIS
AGE.

EPITAPHS.

JOSEPH PARSONS ESQ
Died Nov 29 1722 or (1729)
in the 83^d year of age.

LIDIA
Wife of IOSEP HAWLEY ESQ
who Dy^d Oct 28th 1732 in
ye 76 y^r oF Her Age.

Here lyeth the Body
of
Lie it JOSEPH HAWLEY
who dyed June ye 1 A D 1735
in the 53d year of his age.

This Monument Erected
By JOSEPH CLARKE
To the Memory of
Hon JOSEPH HAWLEY Esq.
who died March 10 1788.

Here lies Mrs REBEKA HAWLEY
who died Jany 2^d 1766 in y^e
81st year of Her age
She was ye widow Mr Joseph
Hawley dec^{sd} at the
right hand of whom she is
intered
And dau^{tr} oF Rev^d
Sol^l Stoddard.

Earth's highest station ends in here he lies,
And dust to dust concludes her noblest song.

EBE^n
EDWARD^s Dy^d
oN OC^r 11 1723 AGE^d
2 yEAE.

MR. WILLIAM Judd
Died May 6
1755 in the
57 year of
his Age.

DEcon Thos Shelden DyD
oN IVAE ye 7th 1775
AGE 63 yEARS.

LYETH
HERE THE BODy oF
IOHN PARSONS ESQ who
Decesed NOVEMBER ye 29
A D 1729 AGED 83
yEARS.

HERE LyETH THE BODy
oF MRS ELISEBETH PAR
SONS RELiCK oF IOSEPH
PARSONS ESQ wHo
DyED MAy ye 11 A D
1736 AGED 89 yEARS.

HERE is BuRiED THE
BODy oF CAPTAIN
EBENEZER PARSONS
who Died July the
1st 1744 IN ye 69th
yEAR of his AGE.

HERE LiES ye BO
Dy oF MR MOSES
PARS *** WHO
DIED IANuARy 3
1745^6 AGED
37 yEARS.

MRS MERCy
WiFE oF CAP.
EBENEZER
PARSONS Di-
ED NOVRM[b] 1st
1753 AGED
68 yEARS.

EuNICE, DAuT[r]
of MOSES PAR
SONS DIED A
PRiL 17 1755
in the 18 yEAR
oF HER AGE.

In Memory of
Mr. BENJAMIN ALVORD
who died Oct°
22[d] 1772
aged 77 years.

Here Lveth the Body
of GIDEON STEBBENS
the SON of LEuf.
BEniAmin & MRS MARy
STEBBENS who DyED
APRIL y° 6th 1734
AGED 20 yEARS.

Mr DANIEL
ALEXANDER
Died April
29th 1752 in
his 42 year.

MARY PERSONS Dy[d]
oN MAy 9 1723
AGED * * *

EPITAPHS.

MARy y^e
WIFE oF SAM
PHELPS DyED
oN NOV^r ye 29
1729 AG^d 44
yEAR.

HERE LIETh THE BODy
oF MR SAMUEL PHELPS
who Died Decemb^r
ye 9th 1745
AGED 65 yERS.

HERE LIES THE
Body of Mr. JOHN
ALEXANDER who
died Decemb^r
the 31st 1733
in y^o 89th year
of his age.

Here lieth the
Body of Mrs SARAI
ALEXANDER who
Died November
the 3d 1732
in ye 83^d year
of her age.

Here lieth the
Body of Mr JOHN
ALEXANDER who
Died June 24
A D 1748-9
aged 77 years.

MRS. REBECKAH CLARK
the daughter of Deacon Josiah
and Mrs. Mary Clark
who joyfully departed
this life April 11th 1776 in the
22^d year of her age.

' A pious youth sleeps here in dust,
' Till raised afresh among the just,
And as she loved her Saviour best
In him she shall forever rest.

EPITAPHS.

| Mr Samuel King Died December 31 A D 1733 in yᵉ 44th year of his age. | Mrs Hannah King Died February 13 A D 1732-3 in yᵉ 40th year of her age. |

IN MEMORy oF
MARTHA yᵉ WIFE
ITHAMER CLARK
Who DIED IunE
THE 27 1744
IN THE 29th yEAR
oF HER AGE * * *

MARY PERSONS
DyED oN SEP 2
1718 AGED * * *
AND * * * DAYS.

Miss. Martha
Daugᵗ of Lieut.
Gideon Lyman
died Februay 28
1753 aged
19 years.

In Memory of
Mrs. Catherine Lyman
Consort of
Gideon Lyman Esq.
who died
March 15 1791
in the 90th year
of her age.

EPITAPHS.

In Memory of
Mr. ZADOK LYMAN
who died
Oct. y° 14th
1754 aged
35 years.

In Memory of
GIDEON LYMAN Esq.
who died April 3d
AD 1775
aged 75 years.

In Memory of
Mrs. SARAH CLARK
Consort of
Mr. William Clark
who died Nov 25 1798
in the 75th year of her age.
'My living friends when this you view,
Remember here is room for you.'
'Jesus can make a dying bed
Feel soft as downy pillows are
While on his breast I lean my head,
And breath my life out sweetly there.'

In Memory of
Mr. EBENEZER PRESCOTT
who died in Dorchester
Oct. 15th 1776
in the 60th year of hir age.
and of
Mrs. JERUSHA PRESCOTT
wife of Mr. Ebenezer Prescott
who died in this Town
Oct. 15th 1779
in the 56th year of her age.
'Life makes the soul dependant on the dust
Death gives her wings to mount above the spheres.'

*3

In Memory of
Mrs. Rachel Barnard
wife of
Mr. Abner Barnard
who died
Dec. 11 1790
in the 61st year
of her age.

In Memory of
Captn Roger Clap
who died Jan 9
Anno Dom 1762
The Memory of the Just is blessed.

Sacred to the Memory
of
Dr Samuel Mather
who died
April 29th 1779
in the 74th year
of his age.

'Corruption, earth and worms,
 Shall but refine this flesh
'Till my triumphant spirit comes,
 'To put in on afresh.
'Hark from the tombs
 'A doleful sound,
'Mine ears attend the cry,
 'Ye living men come view the ground
'Where you must shortly lie.'

In Memory of Mr.
Hezekiah
Wright who died
Sept. 21 1761 in
the 67 year of
his age.

In Memory of
Mrs. Esther Stoddard
The virtuous w^{do} and Relict
of the
Rev^d Mr. Solomon Stoddard
formerly Pastor of the Church
in this Town
who died Feb^{ry} 10th
AD 1736
in the 92^d year of her age.

In Memory of
Mrs. Martha Mather
widow and Relict of
Samuel Mather Esq.
who died
Dec. 2 1785
in the 78th year
of her age.

'Time was like you she life possessed,
'And time shall be when you shall rest.'

In Memory of
Mr. Abner Barnard
who died
of the small pox
Jan. 13 1797
it being his birth day
aged 73 years.

HERE IS BURIED
THE BODy oF MR
IOHN WRIGHT
WHO DIED FEB
8th 1749^8 IN
THE 62 yEAR oF
HIS AGE.

In Memory of
Mrs. ANNE wife of Mr.
Eliphaz Wright who
died Jan. 11th 1785 in
the 34th year of her age.
BOHAN DiED
Sept. 13 1784 aged
8 months ANNE di-
ed Jan. 3d 1785 A
GED 2 yEARS AND
11 MONTHS.

Mrs. HANNAH
WIFE oF Mr.
ABRAHAM MILLER
THEN ye WIFE
oF LIEVT IOHN
PARSONS DECEASED
DIED NOV 9 1758
AGED 77 yERS

Here lies buried the
Body of Mr. JOHN
KINGSLEY who died
July 7th 1742 in
the 76th year of
his age.

Buried here ye Bodies
of JONATHAN & THANKFUL
HUNT children of Deacon
Jonathan Hunt who were
killd by Lightning July
5 1769 In ye 15 yEAR of his
age & ye 7 yEAR of her age.

Death loves a Shining Mark a signal Blow,
A blow which while it creates alarm,
And startles Thousands with a single shaft
* * * * * * *

EPITAPHS.

Captain JOHN POMEROY
who died
March 3 1760
In the 32^d YEAR OF HIS AGE.
DEATH and the GRAVE
without any ORDER.

Here is buried the
Body of MRS SARAH
KINGSLEY who died
June ye 20 1744
in the 77th year
of her age.

In Memory of
SUPLY ye son of
Lieut Suply &
MRS. Elisabth Kings
ley who died
Octo ye 3^d 1736
aged 20 days.

Here lieth the
Body of Lieut
JOHN PARSONS
who died Sept.
4 1746 in the
73 year of his
AGE.

IN MEMORY oF
MRS PHEBE WIFE
oF MR IOHN
WRIGHT ^{W}Ho
DIED NOV 13
1753 IN HER
39 yEAR

EPITAPHS.

In Memory
of the
Hon. John Stoddard Esq.
who was born in
Northampton Feb 11th 1681
and died at Boston
June 19th 1748
in the 67th year of his age.
and entomb^d there
And
In Memory of
his virtuous w^{do} and Relict
M^{dm} Prudence Stoddard
who was born at
Weathersfield March 4th 1699
and died at Northampton
September 11th 1780 and lies
here inter^d and of their infant daughter Hannah Stoddard born
on the 13th Octr 1742 and died the first of Augst
following and lieth at her Mothers feet.

HERE LIES ye BO
Dy oF MOSES
PARSONS who
died January 3
1745-6 aged
37 years.

SACRED to the MEMORY
OF
Col^o SETH POMEROY
who died in the ARMY of
the UNITED STATES at
PEEKSKILL. FEB 19th 1777
IN THE 71st yEAR OF HIS AGE.

Note.—The design on the Monument is two Angels with trum-
pets, holding a cross, in a crown; below, swords crossed, cannon on
each side, and drum and flags with B. G. on them.

EPITAPHS. 35

Mrs Mary the
widow of Ensign
Ebenezer Shel
don Died Nov
10 1767 In the
88th yEAR oF
her AGE.

In Memory of
Mr Edward
Baker who di-
ed March 4th
1758 in ye 73^d
year ol his age.

IN MEMORY of
ENSIGN EBENEZER
SHELDEN WHO
DIED MARCH
ThE 18 A D 1755
AGED 77 yEAR

MRS ABIGAL THE
Consort oF ENSIGN
EBENEZER WELLS oF
DEERFIELD
DIED March 18 1772
AGED 80 yEARS.

IN MEMORY oF
SuPPLY——CLAP
wHo DIED Oct 11
1784
IN THE 63 yEAR oF HIS AGE.
HIS DAuG^r HANNAH
DIED SEP 14 1777 IN
THE 9th yEAR
oF HER AGE.

EPITAPHS.

Sacred to the Memory
of the
REV David Brainerd
A FAiTHFuL AND Laborious
Missionary
to the
Stockbridge, Delaware, and Susquehannah
Tribes of Indians
who died in this Town
Oct 10 1747
Æ 32.

REV. JONATHAN EDWARDS.
The American Divine,
Born
Oct. 5, 1703.
Ordained Colleague Pastor with
Rev. Solomon Stoddard, in this town,
Feb. 15, 1727, Dismissed June 22, 1750.
Died of Small Pox in New Jersey
March 22, 1758.
Rev. Thomas Chalmers, D. D.
The Scotch Divine and Projector of the free Church,
Died of Apoplexy, May 30, 1847, in his
67th year.
"God is Love."

Note.—This monument was erected June, 1850, Just 100 years after his dismissal.

Jerusha
Daughter of
Jonathan and Sarah Edwards
Born April 26 1730
Died Feb 14 1747
(by mistake for 1748)
I shall be satisfied when I awake in thy likeness.

EPITAPHS.

IN Memory oF
MRS MARy CONSORT OF
Col° SETH POMEROy
who died Sept 11th A D 1777
in the 72d yEAR oF HER AGE.

IN MEMORy oF
MR MOSES
KINGSLEy
wHO DIED APRIL
28 1773 IN ye
68 yEAR oF
HIS AGE.

MRS MARy ye WIFE
oF MR MOSES KINg-
SLEy OCTOBER THE
1st SHE DIED A-D
1772 IN ye 66 yEAR
oF HER AGE.

In Memory of Mrs
ELIZABETH HuNT
ThE WIFE oF DEACON
EbENEZER HunT
who died June 5th
1777 AGED 70 yEARS.

HERE LIES ThE Body
oF Deacon
EbENEZER Hunt
who died FEbRy 21
1788 in the 85th yEAR
oF his AGE

The Moments seize ; a moment you may wish when worlds want
wealth to buy.

4

EPITAPHS.

In Memory of
Mrs ELIZABETH the wife
of
Captn ROGER CLAP
who died Augst 20 1767
in y^e 81 yEAR oF HER AGE.

In Memory of Mrs
DORCAS Daugh^{tr}
of Mr Ebenezer &
Mrs Jerusha Clark
who died April
11th 1786 aged
25 year.

Erected by M$_1$. Chauncy Curtis.

In Memory of
Mr EBENEZER EDWARDS
who was instantly killed
by the fall of a tree
on the 21st of Augst 1771
in y^e 44th year of
his age.

In Memory of
Mrs LUCY EDWARDS
widow & Relict of
the late Mr
Ebenezer Edwards
who died August
19 1807 aged 83 years.

" How few whose days amount
" To three score years & ten,
" And all beyond that short amount
* * * * * toil and pain.

EXPERIENCE
WRIGHT Dy^d
oN AVGVT
ye 14 1777 A * * *
NERE 6 y^r
oLD obADIA
DAVGTER.

In Memory of
Cap Noah Wright
who died July 27
AD 1775 in the
76 year of his age.

'Life like the Solar Shadow
'Speeds away from Point
'To Point.
'Tho seeming to stand still
'Thus soon Mans hours are
'up, and we are gone.

In Memory of
Sarah Con
sort of Cap Noah
Wright who died
April 3d AD 1777
in the 77 year
of her age.

This is Erected
To the Memory of
Mrs Miriam Wright
Consort of Ephraim
Wright Esq who died
Jan 2d 1774 in the 53d
year of her age.

EPITAPHS.

Mr Phinehas
The Son of M^r
Joseph Allen
died July 30
1765 in the 20th
year of his age.

Here lies buried
The Body of Jonathan
the only Child of Maj^r
Jonathan and Mrs Sarah
Allen who died
Sep 25 1777
in the 3^d year of
his age.

Sacred to the Memory
of
Maj^r. JONATHAN ALLEN,
who was slain as he
was hunting on the
7th day of Jan., 1780,
Having just entered the
43^d year of his age.

The duties of a Son, of a Brother, and Husband, a Parent, and a faithful and brave OFFICER in the Continental service, were duly discharged by him. He for many years made a public profession of Christianity, and entertained an hope of a Resurection to a glorious Immortality, which did not leave him in the nearest approach to the other world.

On the foot Stone:

Major
JONATHAN ALLEN.
Earth's highest station
Ends in, "Here he lies:"
And "Dust to dust"
Concludes her noblest song.

EPITAPHS. 41

In Memory of
JOSEPH ALLEN
who died Dec 30 1779
Æt 66.
And of ELISABETH (PARSONS)
His wife
who died Jan 10 1800
Æt 84.
Both Exemplary and Eminent Christians. "The Memory of the Just is blessed."
In respect for their virtues, this Monument is Erected by their Grandsons, Solomon and Moses Allen.

In Memory of
Mr ELISHA ALLEN
who died Nov 22 1796
in the 45 year of his age.
"Not he who acts the greatest part,
"But they who act the best,
"Will be the happiest. * * *

ELIJAH ALLEN died Sept.
23, 1830, aged 76.
KEZIAH, wife of
E. Allen, died Jan. 2, 1825,
Æ 69.

HARRIET MARIA,
daughter of Charles J.
and Maria Allen, of
New Haven, Con.,
died at Northampton,
Sept. 24th, 1825,
aged 16 months.

In Memory of
WILLIAM ALLEN, ESQ.
formerly of Boston,
died March 11, 1825,
Aged 84 years.

*4

In Memory of
Mrs Thankful King
who died Jan^ry 17th
1777 in the 35th
year of her age.

In Memory of
Mr Daniel King
who died June
24th 1775
in the 86th year
of his age.

In Memory of Mrs
Mary King the wife
of Mr Daniel King
who died Nov 22^d
1773 in the 83^d year
of her age.

In Memory of Mrs
Mindwell wife of
Mr Samuel Smeed
of Montague who —— * * *
May 10th 1775
in the 57th year
of her age.

In Memory of
Mrs Martha Stoddard
the worthy Consort of
Solomon Stoddard Esq
who Died Oct 20 1772
aged 33.

"My flesh shall slumber in the ground,
"Till the last trumpet's Joyful sound,
"Then burst the Chains with sweet surprize,
"And in my Saviour's image rise.

In Memory of
Mrs EUNICE STODDARD
The worthy Consort of
Solomon Stoddard Esq
who died Jan 22 1797
in the 46 year of her age.
"Her Saviour shall her life restore,
And raise her from her dark abode,
Her Flesh and Soul shall part no more,
But dwell forever near her God.
LET IT BE REMEMBERED
that DAVID their
Infant Son died
April 6 1778 aged 3 Months.

In Memory of
SOLOMON STODDARD, ESQ.
Son of John and Prudence
Stoddard, who died Dec. 19, 1827,
aged 94 years.

Sacred to the Memory of
Miss ESTHER STODDARD, daughter of the
Hon. John Stoddard, and Mrs. Prudence
Stoddard, who died May 27th, 1816,
in the 79th year of her age.
Passing Reader, Emulate her virtues, that your Death may be
tranquil as hers.

In Memory
of Madam SARAH HOOKER,
Relict of the Rev. John Hooker,
who after a long life of
distinguished piety and
usefulness, departed in peace
April 5, A. D. 1817, in the 86 year of
her age.
Heaven owns her friends on this side death, and points them out
to men a lecture silent, but of sovereign power.

EPITAPHS.

Lydia
The wife of
Ensign Josiah Pomeroy
Died
Decemb^r 19 1772
in ye 63 year
of her age.

In Memory of
Mrs Abigal Lyman
wife of
Mr Joseph Lyman
who died
May 1st 1776
in the 75th year
of her age.

" The grave is that home of Man
" Where dwells the Multitude.

In Memory of
Mr Joseph Lyman
who died
March 30th 1763
in ye 64th year
of his age.

" This shall our mouldering members teach,
" What now our senses learn,
" For dust and ashes loudest preach
" Man's infinite concern.

Sacred to the memory of
Mr Elisha Lyman
who departed this life
August 13th 1798
Being in the 65th year
of his age.

" Man departs this earthly scene,
" Ah! never to return,
" No second Spring shall ere revive
" The ashes of the urn.

EPITAPHS.

Mrs HANNAH KING
Died
February ye 13
AD 1732
in ye 40th year
of her age.

Mr SAMUEL KING
Died
December 31
AD 1737 in y^e
44th year of his age.

In Memory of
ENSIGN NOAH STRONG
who Died
June 4th AD 1783
in the 74th year
of his age.

In Memory of
Mrs MARY the wife of
Ensign Noah Strong
who Died
March 16 1771
in ye 66 year
of her age.

In Memory of
Mrs MARTHA CLARK
Relict of
Mr Elihu Clark
who died
March 28th 1795
in the 63^d year
of her age.

"Jesus saith unto her, I am the Resurrection and the life."

Sacred to the Memory
of
Mr S̲e̲l̲a̲h̲ W̲r̲i̲g̲h̲t̲
who died
Dec 17 1786
Æt 64 years.

Also
In Memory of
Mrs E̲s̲t̲h̲e̲r̲ W̲r̲i̲g̲h̲t̲
Relict of
Mr Selah Wright
who died
August 11 1815
Æt 90 years.

In Memory of
Capt J̲o̲h̲n̲
B̲a̲k̲e̲r̲ who di
ed Jan^r 8th 1762
in the 81 year
of his age.

In Memory of
Capt J̲o̲h̲n̲ B̲a̲k̲e̲r̲
who died February
3^d 1802 in the 87th
year of his age.

'Why should we mourn departed friends,
Or shake at death's alarm,
'Tis but the voice that Jesus sends
To call them to his arms.'

M̲r̲s̲ R̲e̲b̲e̲c̲k̲a̲h̲ the
Consort of Captain
John Baker
died June 28th
1774 in the 87th
year of her age.

In Memory of
Mr JONATHAN STRONG
who died April 19th
1797 in the 89th year
of his age.

'The saints are freed from toil and strife,
'And present with the Lord,
'The labours of their mortal life,
'End in a large reward.'

In Memory of
MRS ELISABETH the wife
of Ensign Jonathan Strong
who died June 25
1758 aged 48 years
& 17 days.

Sacred to the Memory
of
DOCT WILLIAM MATHER
who died
April 10th AD 1775
in the
33d year of his age.

Sacred to the Memory
of
MRS EUNICE MATHER
wife of
Mr Elisha Mather
who died
Sept 26th 1776
in the 38th year of her age.

'Her Body here entombed in dust,
'Her pious soul is gone we trust,
'Among the assembly of the just.'

In Memory of
Mr Elisha Mather
who died
March 22 1807
aged 67 years.

The Body of
Jemimi Lyman
widow of the late
Capt William Lyman
is here deposited.
She was born in Northampton
November 1726 & died Feb^y
1785 in the 59th year of her age.

In Memory of
Deacon Ebenezer Pomeroy
who died April the 22^d 1774
in ye 77th yEAR oF his age.

In Memory of
Mr Caleb Strong
who died Feb 13 AD 1776 in
the 66th year of his age.
' Man's home is in the grave,'
' Here dwells the multitude,'
' We gaze around, we read their monuments,'
' We sigh, and while we sigh, we sink.'

In Memory of
Mrs Phebe Strong
the relict of Mr
' Caleb Strong'
who died Jan 5 An Dom
1802.
We loved but not enough the gentle hand that reared us,
Gladly would we now read that softest Friend, a Mother,
Whose mild converse and faithful council we in vain regret.

In Memory of
Mrs Thankful Lewis
Consort of
Mr Nathan Lewis
of Farmington
who died Sept. 18th
1773, in ye 95th
year of her age.

Here lies intered
the remains of
Col. Seth Hunt
who died Dec 28th, 1779,
Ætat 31.
'Why all this toil for triumphs of an hour,
What, tho' we wade in wealth, or soar in fame,
Earth's highest station ends, in ' here he lies,'
And dust to dust concludes her noblest song.'

Here lies intered
The Body of Mr John Hunt
who died Jany 9th 1788,
in the 73^d year of his age.
Also,
Mrs Esther his wife
died March 19, 1787,
in the 65th year of her age.
They exhibited bright patterns of all the conjugal Parental and social virtues. They adorned the doctrines of God our Saviour by pious and holy lives, and died in hopes of a glorious immortality.
'Teach me O parent from on high,
Like them to live, like them to die.'

In Memory of
Mrs Mary Parsons,
wife of Lieut.
William Parsons
who died Nov. 22, 1759,
in ye 66 year of her age.

Sacred to the Memory
of
Lieut William Parsons
who died August the 7th
AD. 1768, in the 78th year
of his age.

While living men my tomb do view,
Remember well here is room for you.

In Memory of
Mr Jonathan
Hall, who died
Nov. 17, 1776,
in the 44th
year of his
AGE.

In Memory of
Capt. William Lyman
who died March 13th, 1774,
in the 59th year of his age.

"The wise and the just, the pious and brave,
"Live in their death, and flourish in the grave."

In Memory of
Mrs Elizabeth wife of
Deac Ebenezer Pomeroy
who died June 10, 1782,
in the 82 yEAR OF HER AGE.

In Memory of
Mr Isaac Garnsey
who died
Feby ye 16, 1767,
in ye 26 year
of his age.

"Christ's dying saints * * * * *

EPITAPHS. 51

This Monument
is erected in
Memory of
Mr. QUARTUS POMEROY,
who died November 5th, 1803,
Aged 68 years.

Rest here blest saint till from his throne
The morning break and pierce the shade.

Here lies the Body of
Mrs ACHSA TURNER Consort of
Mr David Turner
who departed this life Dec 15, 1790,
in the 25th year of her age.

Also
SOFIA TURNER
Their daughter who died
Aug. 7, 1790, aged 3 months and 19 days.

Mrs. ANNA
wife of
Mr. Joseph Clarke,
died on the 22d of May,
Anno Dom 1776,
aged 23 years
and 7 Months.

In Memory of
Mr. TIMOTHY WRIGHT,
who died Nov. 30,
1764, in the 45 year
of his age.
Also of Mrs. ELIZABETH
Relict of Mr. Timothy
Wright, who died
Jan. 17, 1815, in the
90th year of her age.

In Memory of
NOAH WRIGHT, who died March
19, 1816, aged 41 years.
'O glorious hour, O blest abode,
'I shall be near and like my God,
'And flesh, and sense, no more control
'The sacred sorrows of my soul.'

In Memory of
Mr. JAMES HULBERT,
who died April 10, 1767,
in the 80th year of his age.

In Memory of
Mrs. MARY, the wife of
Mr. James Hulbert,
who died June 17, 1760,
in the 63 year of her age.

In Memory of Mrs.
PHEBE POMEROY,
wife of Mr. Quartus Pomeroy who died
May 30th Anno Dom 1776 in the 41st
year of her age.

The Parent kind, whose bounty caused the poor to smile, the obliging neighbour, faithful friend, leaves here her dust to sleep awhile in peace, she liv'd in peace, she dy'd and rests in hope to live again, when Christ her Lord, comes glorify'd to raise his saints, with him to reign.

In Memory of
Supply Clap,
who died
June 20th 1800
in the 34th year of
his age.
Friends and Physicians could not save
This mortal body from the grave,
Nor can the grave confine it here
When Jesus calls it must appear.

In Memory of
Mrs. LUCRETIA CLAP,
wife of Mr. Supply Clap,
who died Sep. 20th, 1795,
in the 26th year of her age.

In Memory of
Mrs. RACHEL POMEROY,
Relict of Mr. Quartus Pomeroy,
who died with an unshaken
faith in Jesus,
Nov. 18, 1826,
Æt 80 years.

In Memory of
Mr. EZRA CLARK
who died July 19, 1788,
in the 73d year of his age.

In Memory of
Mrs. MARTHA CLARK,
Consort of Mr. Ezra Clark
who died Sept. 9, 1803,
aged 86 years.

CLARISSA, wife of
Daniel Stebbins,
Born June 4th, 1767,
Deceased Feburary 26th, 1820,
Blessed are the dead who die in the Lord.

This Stone is near the Town tomb on the east side of the Burying ground about 2 1-2 feet high.

CENOTAPH

OF

DANIEL STEBBINS.

ROWLAND STEBBINS.

	Month.	day.	year.	AGE.
Died in Northampton				
" "	Dec.	14,	1671.	77.

The following descendants died in Springfield.

THOMAS, Eldest Son of
Rowland.   Sept. 23, 1683, 73.
My G. G. G. G. F.

The first JOSEPH Son of Thomas
Died   Oct. 15, 1628, 78.
G. G. G. F.

The second JOSEPH
Drowned   1721, 47.
G. G. F.

The third JOSEPH
Died   March 8, 1793, 88.
G. F.

His wife MARY,
Died   Jan. 9, 1803, 88.
G. M.

The fourth JOSEPH
Died   April   1819, 82.
F.

His wife EUNICE
Died   Nov. 22, 1818, 78.
M.

ROWLAND STEBBINS the supposed ancestor of all the name in America, came from the west of England to Springfield with his Sons John and Thomas about 1636,—removed to Northampton, and there died.   1671.

DANIEL STEBBINS of the 6 generation from THOMAS was Born   April 2, 1766.

In Memory of
Capt. Joseph Cook,
who died June 23, 1788,
in the 62 year of his age.

'Behold and see as you pass by,
'As you are now so once was I,
'As I am now, so you must be,
'Prepare to die, and follow me.

In Memory of
Mrs. LYDIA COOK,
widow and Relict of
Capt. Joseph Cook,
who died March 6th, 1814,
in the 79 year of her age.

In Memory of Mr.
ASA WRIGHT,
who died Nov.
28th, 1786, in the 46th
year of his age.

'Man's home is in the grave,
'There dwell the multitude,
'We gaze around, we read their Monuments,
'We sigh, and while we sigh we sink.'

TIMOTHY EDWARDS DWIGHT,
son of
Josiah and Rhoda Dwight,
Died January 22^{d}, 1807,
aged 7 years.

FRANCIS HENRY,
son of
Josiah and Caroline Dwight,
'who died at sea'
July 23, 1812
aged 22 years.

CLARISSA daughter of
Josiah Rhoda and Dwight,
died Nov. 12, 1820,
aged 3 years.

CAROLINE WILLIAMS,
daughter of
Josiah and Rhoda Dwight,
died Dec. 19, 1813,
aged 15 years.

In Memory of
Miss MARGARETTE DWIGHT,
Died Sept. 5, 1845,
aged 41.

'Father I will that they also whom thou hast given me, be with me, where I am.'

Erected by pupils of the Gothic Seminary to the memory of a much loved teacher.

Sacred to the Memory
of
ELI P. ASHMUN,

At various times a Member of the Councils of the State and Nation, by his native force of Mind, Industry, and probity, he had obtained publick regard, professional eminence and domestick affection, and at the close of life he exhibited the humility and pious submission of a disciple of Christ. He was born June 24, 1770, and died May 10, 1819, in the 49th year of his age.

Why lingers hope around the silent dead,
There is another and a better world.

In Memory of
Mrs. LUCY ASHMUN,
wife of Eli P. Ashmun,
who died Oct. 9th, 1812,
aged 37 years.

EPITAPHS. 57

Sophia W. Ashmun,
eldest daughter of
Eli P. Ashmun, and Lucy his
wife, was born Dec. 11, 1802,
died Aug. 27, 1820,
in the 18th year of her age.

Sacred to the Memory of
Orpha Ashmun,
youngest daughter of
Justice Ashmun, Esq. of Blandford.
And Keziah his wife who died Aug. 17, 1814, aged 28.

The only Monument in Memory of an Indian, is one mile west of the Court House, near a grove of Pines, with the following inscription.

Joseph Mamanach,
Died May y^e * * 1767,
aged 40 years.

Note.—Sally Mammanash, a pious woman, her daughter is living, aged 86, the only Indian in Northampton. Her mother was the sister of Samson Occom, the celebrated Indian preacher.

David Turner,
Died Feb. 11, 1803.
aged 39.
Electa,
His 2d wife
Died April 2, 1850,
aged 83.

In memory of
Mr. Elias Mann,
who died
May 12th, 1825,
in the 75th, year
of his age.
Also 5 Children.
'The Memory of the just is blessed.'

EPITAPHS.

Asenath,
Relict of
Elias Mann,
Died
April 22, 1842,
aged 78.

Justin Cook,
Died
Nov. 1, 1801.
aged 40.
Mary, his
widow,
Died Jan. 15, 1838,
aged 74.

Here lies
Miranda Williams,
the daughter of
Rev. Solomon and
Mrs Mary Williams,
who died
December 25th, 1815,
in the 24th year of
her age.

'My Spirit looks to God alone,
'My Rock and refuge is his throne;
'In all my fears, in all my straits,
'My Soul for his salvation waits.'

In Memory of
Mrs. Mary Williams,
Relict of
Rev. Solomon Williams,
Born Sept. 10, 1756.
Died Feb. 7, 1842, Æ 85 y^{rs}. 5 mos.

'And he saith unto me, write, blessed are they which are called unto the Marriage Supper of the Lamb.'

EPITAPHS. 59

JULIA, daughter of
Rev. Solomon Williams, died
March 10, 1849, aged 65 years.

'And to her was granted, that she should be arrayed in fine linen clean and white.'

Miss
REBECCA PARSONS,
died Jan. 18,
1828, aged
51 years.

' Unveil thy bosom faithful tomb,
' Take this new treasure to thy trust,
' And give their sacred relicks, room
' To slumber in the silent dust.'

LEMUEL CLARK,
Died
May 27, 1837,
aged 73.

In Memory of
Mrs. LUCRETIA CLARK,
wife of
Mr. Lemuel Clark,
who died
Nov. 20, 1823,
aged 55 years.

' Stranger, if by chance or feeling led,
' Upon this hallowed turf thy foot-steps tread,
'Turn from the contemplation of this sod,
' And think on her whose spirit rests with God.'

In Memory of
Capt. JOSEPH COOK,
who died Feb. 14, 1814.

' Friends nor Physcians could not save,
' This Mortal body from the grave.'

EPITAPHS.

In Memory of
Mr. Joseph Cook,
who died July 12, 1825,
aged 34 years.

In Memory of
Deacon Noah Cook,
who died Jan. 6, 1773,
in ye 85 year of his age.

Seth Dickinson Clark,
died Nov. 1, 1816,
aged 7 years.
Lemuel Coleman Clark,
Died Aug. 9, 1807,
aged 1 month, children of
Mr Lemuel and Mrs. Lucretia Clark.

Elijah Cook,
died July 1, 1827,
aged 57 years.

Here lies Intered,
The Body of Mrs. Abigail, wife of
Deac^n. Noah Cook,
who died Dec. 27, 1766.
in y^e
75 year of her age.

Rev. Wm. .M Doolittle,
aged 27,
Pastor of the Baptist Church
Northampton, Died Feb. 12, 1842.
' Weep not my friends, weep not for me, all is well,
' All now is peace and joy divine,
' And heaven and glory now are mine,
' O, hallelujah to the Lamb, all is well.'
' I have fought the good fight,
' I have kept the faith.'

EPITAPHS. 61

EMELINE COOK,
daughter of Mr. Elijah and
Mrs. Esther Cook, died
Dec. 25, 1818, aged 8 years.
' My parents dear weep not for me,
' When in this yard my grave you see ;
' My time was short and blest was He
' That call'd me to eternitie.'

ENOS,
The son of Mr. Aaron Cook,
Died Oct. 31, 1771,
Aged 13 years and 8 months.

HANNAH,
Wife of Enos Cook,
Died Oct. 4, 1840,
aged 61.

JOHN LA
NKTON Dy E^d
oN IEN^r ye 26
1728 AG^d 46 yE^{a}R.

ZERUAH
wife of
William Clark, Jun.
Died
June 5, 1842,
aged 46 years.

CHARLOTTE,
Daughter of
William and
Zeruah Clark,
Died
Aug. 14, 1845,
Æ 20 years.

CHARLES STARKWEATHER, Esq.
died July 9th 1843,
aged 84,
ROXANA
his wife
Died
Jan. 5, 1847,
aged 77.

This Stone
is erected to the
Memory of Mrs.
PATTY STARKWEATHER,
wife of Mr.
Charles Starkweather,
who died May 9th 1804,
aged 42 years.
'The dust returns to dust
The Soul remains secure in her existence.'

> T O D D.

William Todd,
Died
June 33, 1846,
Æ 67.

Mrs. MARY, wife of
Mr. Phineas Parsons,
Died Aug. 8, 1823,
in the 70th year of her age.

As a wife and mother few have excelled her in the tender solicitude for the happiness of her family.
'Blessed are the dead which die in the Lord, that they may rest from their labors, and their works do follow them.'

In Memory of
Mr. Phineas Parsons,
who Died Feb. 7, 1825,
aged 57 years.

Mr. Phineas Parsons Junr.
Died Feb. 23, 1818, aged 31 years.

By his amiable disposition he was endeared to the domestic circle, an affectionate Husband, a tender Father, a dutiful Son, and a pleasant Brother.

Miss Nancy Parsons,
Died April 21, 1811, Æ 28 years.

She early professed her faith in Christ, and exemplified the christian character in the various relations and circumstances of life.
'Mourning friends adieu,
Here I retire from mortal sight to see my Saviour face to face.'

Nancy,
wife of Benjⁿ. North,
Born Jan. 2, 1807,
Died Sep. 2, 1844,
'Jacob set a pillar on Rachels grave.'
Hannah Annetta,
daughter of Ben and Nancy
North, died Jan. 10, 1841,
Æ 3 years and 8 mo.
Also an Infant,
Born Feb. 28,
Died March 6, 1842.

In Memory of
Miss Abigal Graves,
Who died Jan. 16, 1819,
Aged 31 years.

'The wintery blasts of death kill not the buds of virtue. No, they spread beneath the heavenly beams of brighter Suns, through endless ages, into higher powers.'

In Memory of
Elisha Graves,
Who died April 11, 1826,
Aged 68 years.

Catherine,
Relict of Mr. Elisha Graves,
Died June 20, 1833,
Aged 79.

In Memory of
Mr. Edward Graves,
Son of Mr. Elisha and Mrs. Catherine Graves,
Who died Sept. 28, 1823,
In the 25th year of his age.
'Death cannot make our souls afraid,
'If God be with us there,
'We may walk through the darkest shade,
'And never yield to fear.'

In Memory of
Mr. Daniel Warner,
who died Feb. 29, 1812,
aged 57 years.
Also
Mrs. Phœbe Warner,
Consort of Mr. Daniel Warner,
died March 20, 1817,
aged 57 years.

Sophia H. Lyman,
Widow of
Hon. J. H. Lyman,
and daughter of
Judge Hinckley,
Died April 6, 1839,
Aged 51 years.

In Memory of
Jonathan H. Lyman,
An enterprising and useful
Citizen, of high intellectual
Powers, and accomplished education,
Who Died
distinguished alike
by private affection and Public Regard,
Nov. 3, 1825.

William Bolter,
Born Feb. 11, 1766,
Died April 27, 1841.

John Breck Esq.,
Died Feb. 26, 1827,
aged 56 years.

'Great day of dread decision and despair,
'At thought of thee each sublunary wish
'Lets go its eager grasp, and drops the world,
'And catches at each reed of hope on heaven.'

This Humble Stone
Is erected Sacred to the Memory of
Mrs. Electa Breck,
wife of Mr. John Breck,
who departed this life
April 16, 1800,
in the 31st year of her age.

'Few are our days, those few we dream away,
'Sure is our fate, to moulder in the clay,
'Rise Immortal Soul above thine earthly fate,
'Time yet is thine, but soon it is too late.'

"Clarissa,"
wife of John Breck, Esq.
Died at "Hartford, Con.,"
Dec. 6th, 1831,
Æ 53.

In Memory of
Mr. THEODORE BRECK,
Son of the late Robert Breck, Esq ,
and Mrs. Rachel Breck,
who died February 17th, 1805,
aged 23 years.
'Nipp'd by the chilling hand of death,
' A lovely flower here withering lies,
' The Mortal part is lodg'd beneath,
' The Spirit mounted to the skies.'

This Humble Stone
Is erected to the Memory of
Mrs. SARAH POMEROY,
the wife of Capt. Seth Pomeroy,
who died Augst 10th, 1801,
aged 26 years.
Also their Infant, aged 14 days.

In Memory of
Mrs. SARAH HUNT,
wife of Doct. Ebenezer Hunt,
who died August 12th, 1803,
aged 59 years.
' How populous, how vital is the grave,
' This is Creation's Melancholy vault,
' Where change shall be no more.'

Hon. EBENEZER HUNT, M. D.,
died Decr 26, A. D. 1820,
aged 76 years.

A life devoted to the faithful discharge of Public Offices, Professional duties, and Domestic Charities, adorned with Christian graces, and cheered by Christian hopes, speaks his Eulogy, and constitutes his Memorial, ' Hic Requiescit.'

ABNER HUNT,
Born Aug. 27, 1768,
Died Aug. 20, 1841.

EPITAPHS. 67

SARAH,
Wife of Abner Hunt,
Born Sept. 16, 1772,
Died March 4, 1827.

In Memory of
WM. KING HUNT,
Son of Doct. Ebenezer and Mrs. Sarah Hunt,
who died Jany 27th, 1795,
in the 17th year of his age.
'This gloomy prison waits for you,
'When ere the summons come.'

In Memory of
Miss ELISABETH HUNT,
Daughter of Doct. Ebenezer
and Mrs. Sarah Hunt,
who died Feby 8th, 1797,
aged 14 years.
'Be ye also ready.'

In Memory of
Mr. WILLIAM CLARK,
who died Dec. 29, 1807,
aged 87 years.
'The memory of the Just shall be blessed.'

Died April 7, 1789,
Mr. JOSIAH CLARK,

He was the youngest of 6 sons and 5 daughters, and survived them; from the 5 sons have descended 1158 lineal heirs, 925 were living at his death. 'With long life will I satisfy him and show him my salvation.'

In Memory of
Mrs. MARY CLARK,
wife of Deacon Josiah Clark,
who died March 3, 1797,
in the 72 year of her age.
'My flesh and my heart faileth, but God is the strength of my portion forever.'

In Memory of
Deacon JOSIAH CLARK,
who died Nov. 16, 1808, in the
88th year of his age.

'Our Fathers where are they ? and the prophets do they live forever ?'

BENJAMIN TAPPAN,
Died January 29, 1831,
aged 83 years.
George an infant son
Died Oct. 30, 1793.

'Jesus said unto her I am the resurrection and the life, He that believeth in me though he were dead yet shall he live, and whosoever liveth and believeth in me shall never die, believeth thou this ?'

Mrs. SARAH TAPPAN,
wife of
Benjamin Tappan, Esq.
Died March 26, 1826, aged 78.

'Blessed are the dead, that die in the Lord, for they rest from their labors, and their works do follow them.'

SOLOMON WILLIAMS,
Born
July 25, 1752,
Lived
as Pastor of the church of Christ,
In Northampton,
56 years and 5 months.
HIS SPIRIT
ASCENDED
in sweet peace to the Upper Sanctuary
on the morning of the Sabbath,
Nov. 9, 1834.

In Memory of
Mrs. Elizabeth Phœnix,
wife of Alexander Phœnix,
and daughter of Benjamin and
Sarah Tappan, who died May 30,
1819, aged 28 years.

In her death the church of Christ to which she united herself at the early age of sixteen, has lost an exemplary member; the poor a kind and sympathzing Friend; the social circle a bright ornament, and her surviving relatives an example of loveliness and excellence, in all the duties and relations of private life which will be long and most affectionately remembered.

Joseph,
son of Caleb, and
Hepzibah Hannum,
Died April 15th, 1847,
aged 22.

'Let not your heart be troubled; ye believe in God believe also in me. In my Father's house are many mansions; if it were not so, I would have told you. I go to prepare a place for you.'

'HOPE'
Eliza Anne,
wife of
John Hannum,
Died Aug. 24, 1849,
aged 35.

" As a vision, as a dream of the night,
" The last ray of sunlight upon the wave,
" So fades all earthly hopes.
" Beautiful but Oh! how transitory
" Let us not cling to things of earth,
" For all that is earthly fades away,
" But seek some more substantial treasures,
" Even those that shall endure forever."

Sophia, daughter of
Mr. Spencer and Mrs. Sophia Clark,
Died Sep. 20, 1832,
aged 1 year and 8 months.

SARAH J. BREED,
wife of
Rev. Wm. Allen,
Died Feb. 25, 1848,
aged 58 years.
'Be thou faithful unto death, and I will give thee a crown of life.'

ELLEN WHEELOCK,
only child of
Rev. John Wheelock Allen,
Died June 27, 1841, aged 8 months.

WILLIAM,
son of
Rev. J. W. Allen, of Wayland,
Died Sep. 7, 1842, aged $4\frac{1}{2}$ months.

CHARLES RICE,
son of Rev. J W. Allen,
Died Dec. 20, 1849, aged $2\frac{1}{2}$ months.

MARIA,
daughter of Rev. E. Hopkins,
Died Sept. 1, 1843, aged 9 days.

[The following is on the grave stone of Wm. Allen, another child of Rev. E. Hopkins.]

WILLIE,
Born Jan. 2, 1845,
God took him April 9, 1848.
"He shall have thee, my own, my beautiful, my undefiled, and thou shalt be His child."

HUNT.

'Not Lost but gone before.'

EPITAPHS.

Martha H. Hunt,
Born April 7, 1825,
Died April 5, 1847.

Ebenezer Hunt,
Born March 11, 1775,
Died June 9, 1835.

Maria L Hunt,
Born May 13, 1813,
Died Nov. 10, 1844.

John Hunt,
Born Feb. 20, 1821,
Died April 16, 1823.

Samuel H. Hunt,
Born June 12, 1819,
Died April 23, 1845.

David Hunt, M. D.
Counselor M. M. S.
Died July 8, 1837,
Æ 64.

Wealthy Hunt,
wife of David Hunt,
Died Sept. 25, 1838,
Æt 61.

Frances A. Hunt,
Died Aug. 24, 1838,
Æ 20.

In Memory of
Wealthy Hunt,
Daughter of Mr. David and Mrs. Wealthy Hunt,
who died Aug. 24, 1802, aged 3 years.

HENSHAW FAMILY TOMB.

Hon. Samuel Henshaw,
Died at Northampton, March 11th, 1809.
Æ LXV. YRS.
Francis Aurelia,
Wife of Hon. C. A. Dewey,
Died at Williamstown, July 20th, 1821,
Æ XXIV. YRS.
Eliza,
Daughter of Hon. Samuel and Martha Henshaw,
Died Feb. 20th, 1823,
Æ XXIX YRS.
Louisa Augusta,
Wife of Dr. Charles Beck,
Died Feb. 23, 1830,
Æ XXX YRS.
Martha,
Relict of Hon. Samuel Henshaw,
Died May 27th, 1842,
Æ LXXXVI. YRS and 11 months.

ANSEL WRIGHT'S FAMILY TOMB.

Children of Ansel Wright.
Elizabeth M. C. Wright,
Died April 1, 1838, aged 10 years.
Asahel Wright,
Died Sept. 10, 1840, aged 4 years.
Asahel Wright,
Died Feb. 3, 1844, aged 3 years.
Henry Wright,
Died Dec. 8, 1845, aged 1 year and 8 months.
Harriet Wright,
Died Dec. 5, 1849, aged 5 years and 8 months.

EPITAPHS.

Elizabeth, wife of
Ansel Wright, died
Sept. 10th, 1848, aged 44 years.

In Memory of
Mary, the wife
of Nathaniel Edwards,
who died Sept. 16th,
1819,
in the 69th year of
her age.
' Life how short,
' Eternity how long.

Mr. Nathaniel
Edwards,
Died March 13, 1832,
aged 82.

In Memory of
Capt'n James Dickenson,
who died July 12th 1824,
in the 45th year of his age.
' All, All, is right by God ordained or done, who but God resumed the Friends He gave.'

This Monument
is erected to the
Memory of
Mr. Job White,
who departed this life
Feb. 12, 1807,
aged 54 years.
also of
Lewis White, their son
who Died January 24, 1804,
aged 17 years.

Elizabeth, daughter of
William and Rebecca Edwards,
died Jan. 29, 1807,
aged 1 Month.

Sacred to the Memory of
Mr. Josiah Dickenson,
who died Jan. 17, 1812,
aged 62 years.

"One eye on death, and one full fixed on heaven, becomes a mortal and immortal man."

Sacred to the Memory of
Mrs. Wealthy Dickenson,
wife of
Mr. Josiah Dickenson
who died June 23, 1812,
aged 59 years.

"Heaven gives us Friends to bless the present scene, resumes them to prepare us for the next."

In Memory of
Seth Hopkins Dickenson,
who died March 21st, 1805,
aged 23 years.

In Memory of
Caroline Dickenson,
who died November 7, 1810,
aged 24 years.

'This is the end of man, prepare for it, prepare to die and meet your God.'

Mr. Cotton Dickenson,
died Jan. 21, 1826,
aged 72 years.

Olive, wife of
Cotton Dickenson,
died Sept. 10, 1844.
aged 89.

Asahel Pomeroy, Esq.
died March 22, 1833, in the
84th year of his age.

Mrs. Hannah Pomeroy,
wife of Asahel Pomeroy,
died Sep. 28th, 1812,
aged 58 years.

In Memory of
Mrs. Susannah, wife of
Asahel Pomeroy,
who died January 26, 1826,
aged 69 years.

Here is intered
The Body of
Mrs. Miriam Pomeroy,
Consort of
Mr. Asahel Pomeroy,
who died July 10th, 1793,
in the 41st year of her age.

" A consort tender and a parent dear,
" To none an enemie, to all sincere,
" She joyed with good, the needy to supply,
" And wipe the fading drops from miseries eye,
" The balm of consolation to impart,
" And heal the bruises of the broken heart,
" Cheerfully she lived, and on the bed of death
" Kissing submisively the rod,
" She yielded up her breath."

Lucretia Pomeroy,
Daughter of Asahel Pomeroy,
Died Sep. 22, 1847.

Sacred
To the Memory
of
Miss JUDITH POMEROY,
Daughter of Mr. Asahel
and Mrs. Miriam Pomeroy,
who died
Jan. 20th, 1804,
Æt 20 years.

In Memory of
DAVID L DEWEY,
who died in Northborough,
Feb. 15, 1821, aged 32 years.

"Our days are as the grass,
Or like the morning flower,
If one sharp blast sweeps o'er the field
They wither in an hour."

In Memory of
Mr. LUTHER HUNT,
who died Aug. 28th 1817,
aged 46 years.

"Heaven gives us friends to bless the present scene,
"Resumes them to prepare us for the next."

Four children of Mr. Luther, and Mrs. Eunice Hunt.
LUTHER, died Dec. 4th, 1825,
aged 11 years.
MEDAD, died Sept. 16, 1802,
aged 3 years.
Two Infants died Oct. 23, 1801.

SUSAN, daughter of
Luther and Eunice Hunt,
Born May 7th, 1813,
Died Dec. 28, 1832.

EPITAPHS.

Frederick Hunt,
Died Oct. 9, 1831, Æ 33 years.

To the dear Memory of
Mrs. Abigal Lyman,
Consort of
Erastus Lyman, Esq.
who died
Feb. 18th, 1803,
Æt 24.

"She was a woman with lively good sense and ease,
"And always sure her friends to please,
"For every social virtue form'd."

Possessed of an aimable disposition, with a cultivated mind and understanding, charity and all the delicate virtues, of her sex. In a time of youth and health, she dedicated herself by a public and solemn covenant to the service of the Blessed God, and in his presence as her friends have reason to believe, her unembodied Spirit now adores and is happy.

In Memory of
Mr. John King,
who died
May 14, 1806, in the 77th,
year of his age.

In Memory of
Mrs. Rachel King,
wife of
Mr. John King,
who died June 14th,
1798, in the 56th, year
of her age.

Mrs. Hannah W. Flint,
wife of J. H. Flint,
Died June 16, 1821,
aged 34 years.

This erected to
The Memory of
Ephraim Wright, Esq.
who died Jan. 25th,
1794, in the 82d year,
of his age.

"Both old and young who view this tomb,
"Remember here for you is room."

Sacred to the
Memory of
Mr. HENRY LYMAN,
Merchant of Montreal,
son of the late
Elisha Lyman
of this town,
who died at Burlington, Vt.
Sept. 20, 1809,
Ætat 21 years.

Died March 24, 1820,
MOSES WRIGHT, Esq
aged 68 years.

In the various relations of domestic life he was constant, faithful, and affectionate. As a citizen, he was beloved and respected by an extensive acquaintance, as a professor of the religion of Jesus Christ, his example was worthy of imitation.
'Tis but a few whose days amount to three score years and ten.'

In Memory of
Mrs. DOROTHY HINCKLEY,
wife of Samuel Hinckley,
who died Aug. 26, 1802,
in the 44th, year of her age.

The occupation dearest to her heart was to encourage goodness, and her eye was meek and gentle, a smile played on her lips, and in her speech was heard maternal sweetness, dignity and love.

EPITAPHS.

Hon. SAMUEL HINCKLEY,
Died June 15, 1840, aged 83.

In Memory of
DOLLY ANN HINCKLEY,
the daughter of Samuel
Hinckley, Esq. and Mrs. Dorothy
his wife, who died
Sep. 6th, 1801,
aged 2 years and 6 Months.

In Memory of
DOLLY HINCKLEY,
Daughter of Mr. Samuel and
Mrs. Dolly Hinckley, who
died Jan. 28th, 1798,
aged 2 years.

Here lies the body of
PHEBE ELIZABETH HINCKLEY,
daughter of Samuel Hinckley, Esq.
and Dorothy his wife,
who died Sep. 1st, 1801,
aged 11 Months.

GEORGE HINCKLEY,
son of Samuel and Dorothy Hinckley,
died Sep. 22^{d}, 1818,
in the 28th, year of his age.

He was educated at Yale College, and had commenced the practice of Law, in the midst of the most flattering prospects of happiness to himself and usefulness to others. Disease arrested his progress and Death removed him from his friends, who loved him living and will continue to lament him until memory shall be lost in oblivion.

Vive, memor, quam
Sis aevi brevis.

Thomas Lyman,
died April 15, 1845,
Æ 88.

Miss Parces Lyman,
died April 19, 1826,
Æt 55 years.

In Memory of
Hon. Elijah H. Mills,

Distinguished for a long succession of years, by his ability and eloquence at the bar, his enlightened patriotism, and his extensive beneficial influence as a member of the state and national governments.

who died in the faith of the Gospel,
May 5th, 1829, Æt 52.

Sacred to the Memory of
Mrs. Sarah Mills,
wife of
Elijah Hunt Mills, Esq.
and daughter of the
Hon. Ebenezer Hunt, and Mrs. Sarah Hunt,
who died Oct. 2^{d}, 1802,
in the 23^{d} year of her age.

'The soul looks through the gloomy portals of the grave,
'To happier scenes of Immortality.'

In Memory of
George Francis, son of
Elijah Hunt Mills,
and Harriet his wife,
who died May 25th, 1827,
in the 6th year of his age.

'Weep not for those whom the veil of the tomb,
In life's happy morning hath hid from our eyes,
Ere sin threw a blight o'er the Spirits young bloom,
Or earth had profaned, what was born for the skies.'

EPITAPHS.

Here are intered
The remains of LEWIS
BUTLER, 2^d son of Simeon
and Mary Butler, who died
Feb. 16, 1818, aged 18.

"Weep not for me my dangers all are past,
I've run the race and gained the goal at last,
I've left the cumbrous load of flesh behind. * * *

In Memory of
MARY ANN BUTLER,
eldest child of Simeon and
Mary Butler, who died Sep.
23^d, 1802, in the 8th, year
of her age.

Emblem of innocence thy placid mind knew no rough passion, nor a thought unkind. Bright were our hopes, we mourn to find them vain but God is just and * * * * *

EDWARD BUTLER,
Died July 13, 1849,
aged 52.

WILLIAM BUTLER,
Died March 9, 1831,
aged 68 years.

MARY,
Third daughter of
Mr. William and Mrs. Huldah
Butler, died July 3^d, 1800,
aged 8.

WILLIAM, son
Mr. William and Mrs. Huldah Butler,
Died Sep. 7th, 1802,
aged 15 Months.

JOHN BROWN,
son of Mr. William and
Mrs. Huldah Butler, died
July 5th, 1811,
aged 21 Months.

DANIEL BUTLER,
Died Sep 14, 1833,
aged 65 years.

Under this Stone
rest the remains of
Mrs. ANNA BUTLER,
wife of
Mr. Daniel Butler,
and daughter of John and
Mrs. Mary Welsh, of Boston,
who departed this life
May 9th, 1801, aged 32 years.

Those who knew her not, may learn from this Monumental Stone, that her virtues have rendered her memory precious to her bereaved partner. The sight of it will excite a tender recollection of her worth in the bosoms of those who knew her.

In Memory of
Mrs. MARY BUTLER,
wife of Mr. Simeon Butler,
who died March 1, 1829,
aged 55 years.

Sweet peace and heavenly hope and humble joy, divinely shone on her enraptured soul and crowned her for the skies.

SIMEON BUTLER,
Died Nov. 7, 1847,
aged 77 years.
'The Lord our righteousness.'

In Memory of
Mr. HERVEY TILLOTSON,
who died Sep. 12, 1813,
in the 31 year of his age.

In Memory of
Rev. HENRY LYMAN,
son of
Theodore and Susan W. Lyman,
a Missionary of the
American Board
who with his associate
Rev. Samuel Munson,
suffered a violent death
from 'The Battahs' in Sumatra,
June 28, 1834,
aged 24.

"We are more than conquerors."

In Memory of
Mr. ABNER BARNARD,
who died
Jan. 11, 1806,
in the 23^d year
of his age.

'Lord I commit my soul to thee.'

ENOS KINGSLEY,
died Nov. 6, 1845,
aged 75.

REBECCA,
wife of
Enos Kingsley,
died Jan. 27, 1823,
aged 47.

In Memory of
Mrs. RUTH DIXON,
wife of Mr. John Dixon,
of Killingly, Con.
who departed this life
Aug. 22, 1811, in the 34 year of
her age.

ARTHUR FRANCIS,
son of William H. and
Sarah B. Stoddard,
died Nov. 27, 1839,
aged 18 months.

WILLIAM BRADISH,
eldest son of William H.
and Sarah B. Stoddard,
died Nov. 1842, aged
7 years and 7 months.
"Is it well with the child? and she answered it is well."

"Thy son liveth."
DAVID TAPPAN,
son of William H.
and Sarah B. Stoddard,
died Oct. 21, 1848,
aged 5 years.
His soul was gentle as a lamb.

INGOLS.

In Memory of Miss ABIGAL INGOLS,
Daughter of Mr. James and
Mrs. Mary Ingols, who died * * * 11, 1826,
Æt 23 years.
There was a time, that time has past,
When youth, I bloom'd like thee,
A time will come, is coming fast,
When thou shalt fade like me.

EPITAPHS. 85

Timothy Edwards,
son of
Josiah and Rhoda Dwight,
Died May 29th, 1833, aged 25 years.

Hannah Worthington,
daughter of
Josiah and Rhoda Dwight,
died Sep. 17, 1829,
aged 17 years.

William Harris,
son of
Josiah and Caroline Dwight,
who perished in the wreck
of the Albion on the Irish Coast,
April 22d, 1822, aged 29 years.

This tribute of affection is inscribed by her who occupied the place of Mother, to whom and her children his conduct was ever a chaste and touching example of filial and Fraternal love, but yet remembering that the parting sigh appoints the just to slumber not to die.

The starting tear I check'd,
I kiss'd the Rod
And not to earth resigned them,
But to God.

In Memory of
Josiah Dwight, Esq.
who was born Sep.
17, 1767, and died March 8, 1821.

In the faith and hope of the glorious Gospel of the Blessed God.

Thomas, son of
Josiah and Rhoda Dwight,
Died Oct. 1815, aged 5 years.

Hannah Buckminster,
Daughter of
Josiah and Rhoda Dwight,
Died Feb. 16, 1814,
aged 2 years.

Charles Hooker, died
May 13th, 1833, aged 36 years.

In Memory of
Miss Abigal Welsh Butler,
daughter of Daniel and Anna
Butler, who died Sep. 4,
1822, aged 24 years.

Faith with a bright unwavering eye
Points with a smile above the sky,
And wafts the mourner to that shore,
Where mourning friends shall part no more.

Also in Memory of
Mr. Charles Parker Butler,
Son of Daniel and Anna Butler,
who died at the Bay of
St. Louis Sept. 15 1820,
aged 26 years.

Though strangers only lingered by
And mutely watched the strugling sigh,
Yet nature's if not friendship's tear,
Shall nightly wet the distant bier.

In Memory of
Mr. Joseph
Bartlet,
who died August 3, 1755,
aged 73 years.

Benjamin
Bartlet, Died
Aug. 23, 1762,
in the 62 year
of his age.

Note.—This stone is broken, and in three pieces, and lays 22 yards east of the Henshaw tomb.

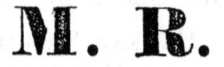

M. R.

Note.—This is a rough stone, 18 inches square, 60 feet east of Lieut. Wm. Clark's grave.

EPITAPHS. 87

UPHAM.

DAVID GORHAM,
Child of
Tim° & Julia U. Wood, of New York,
Died 11th Sept., 1822,
aged 2 years.

Mrs. RACHEL LANGFORD,
Died Dec. 30, 1780,
in the 24th year of her age.

Mrs. MINDWELL,
Relict of Capt'n Moses Lyman,
Died May 25, 1780,
in the 88th year of her age.

In Memory of
Mr. JONATHAN STRONG,
who died Dec. 18th, 1803,
in the 67th year of his age.

In Memory of
Mrs. RACHEL STRONG,
Wife of Mr. Jonathan Strong,
who died Dec. 21, 1817,
in the 80th year of her age.

B. L.

NOTE.—This stone is 20 feet north of Hon. Joseph Hawley's Monument.

EPITAPHS.

D. L.

Note. — This is an unwrought stone, 18 inches high, 24 wide, 60 feet south of the pine tree, on the hill.

In Memory of
Mrs. MARTHA CLARK,
Wife of Mr. Aaron Clark,
who died March 13, 1803, aged 50 years.

HEAR LIES
intered the body of
ELDER PRESERVED CLAPP,
oF Northampton,
who died September the 22, 1720,
in the 77 year of his age.

Note.—This stone is on the hill, near the pine tree.

HEAR LIES
intered the body of
Mrs. SARAH CLAPP,
of Northampton,
who died Oct. 4, 1716,
in the 66 year of her age.

In Memory of	In Memory of
Mr. ELIPHAZ CLAP,	Mrs. RACHEL, ye wife of
who died July 20, 1783,	Mr. Eliphaz Clap,
aged 71 years.	who died Jan. 11, 1762,
	in ye 41 year of her age.

In Memory of
Capt. ELISHA POMEROY,
who died Jan'y 26, 1762, in ye 41 year of his age.
   " A law eternal does decree,
   That all things born shall mortal be."

DAVID JUDD,
Born April 12, 1771,
Died May 21, 1827.

SARAH JUDD,
Wife of David Judd,
Born Nov. 26, 1774,
Died Oct. 10, 1826.

In Memory of
DAVID JUDD,
Son of Mr. David and Mrs. Sally Judd,
died Oct. 26, 1807,
aged 17 months and 11 days.
Also an infant daughter,
died Oct. 2d, 1801, aged 1 day.

SPENCER JUDD,
Died Oct. 30, 1832, aged 32 years.

ELIZA S. JUDD,
Wife of Spencer Judd,
died June 13, 1830, aged 29.

CHARLES SPENCER JUDD,
their son, died Oct. 29, aged 5 years.

NOTE.—Mr. Judd, wife and child, died in Springfield, and were interred in the "Old Burying Ground." Their remains were removed and re-interred in this place, May, 1848, by Thomas Bridgman.

SARAH H. WELLS,
Wife of Samuel Wells,
and daughter of Hon. Jonathan Leavitt,
of Greenfield,
Died Jan'y 29th, 1837,
aged 40 years.

In Memory of
Mrs. RACHEL RUSSELL,
Consort of Mr. John Russell,
who died February 10, 1810, aged 27 years.

EPITAPHS.

Laura,
Wife of John Russell,
died Feb. 9, 1826, Æ 38.

"Jacob set a pillar on Rachel's grave."

In Memory of
Miss Cordelia Snow,
Daughter of Mr. Ralph and Mrs. Theodocia Snow,
Born Nov. 12th, 1798,
Died Aug. 16th, 1824.

And if we believe that Jesus died and rose again, even so them also which sleep in Jesus will God bring with him.

Here Lyes the Body of
Samuel Curtis,
who died the 24 of IuLy, in the year 1721,
in the 73 year of his age.

Note.—This Monument is on the hill, and in a good state of preservation.

Hon. Joseph Lyman,
Born Oct. 22, 1767, died Dec. 11, 1847.

In Memory of
Mrs. Elizabeth Lyman,
Consort of Joseph Lyman,
and daughter of Hon. Samuel Fowler,
of Westfield,
who died July 16th, 1808.

Also of their Daughter,
Frances,
who died at Medford,
Jan'y 11th, 1809, Atat 12.

Death kills not the buds of virtue,
No, they spread * * * * *

EPITAPHS.

Lydia,
Dau' of Lieut. Enock and Mrs. Nancy Clarke,
died June 15, 1773,
aged 2 years and 4 months.

Mrs. Lucinda Clarke,
Died Jan'y 25, 1840, aged 74.

Christopher Clarke,
Died Sept. 28th, 1838, aged 45.

Elizabeth W.,
Dau' of F. W. and L. B. Clarke,
died Sept. 28, 1848, aged 8 years.

Death came with friendly care,
The opening bud to heaven conveyed,
And bade it blossom there.

John Phillips,
Son of John and Prudence Clarke,
Born Dec. 17, 1828, died Oct. 22, 1831.

Sarah W. Whitney,
Wife of Josiah D. Whitney,
and daughter of Rev. Payson Williston,
died July 1, 1833, Æ 33.

Earth has her dust, friends her memory, and the Redeemer her Spirit.

William Dwight,
Son of J. D. and S. W. Whitney,
died April 3, 1826, aged 7 weeks.

Margaretta,
Daughter of J. D. and S. W. Whitney,
died June 23, 1836,
aged 7 years.

ALICE CLARISSA,
Daughter of J. D. and C. J. Whitney,
died March 25, 1840, aged 6 months.

ELLEN DOUGLASS,
Daughter of J. D. and C. J. Whitney,
died July 27, 1846, aged 18 months.
Jesus call'd a little child unto him.

This Monument, erected by a friend,
To the Memory of
RICHARD SMITH,
Son of Mr. Noadiah and Mrs. Abigal Pease,
died March 31, 1812,
aged 9 months and 12 days.
" Frail, smiling solace of an hour,
So soon our transient comforts fly,
And pleasures only bloom to die."

In Memory of
FANNY,
Daughter of the late Mr. Joseph Hunt Breck,
and Mrs. Abigal Breck,
who died July 8th, 1802,
aged 8 years, 1 month and 9 days.
"An opening bud, a morning flower,
Cut down and withered in an hour."

ACHSA MARIA,
Daughter of Cephas and Achsa Clark,
died Feb. 15, 1845, Æ 42 years.
A. M.,
Dau. of C. and A. Clark,
died Oct. 8, 1821, Æ 8 mos.

Here lies deposited the body of
MARTIN BRECK,
Son of John and Electa Breck,
who died Dec. 12th, 1797.

This humble Stone is erected
Sacred to the memory of
Mr. WILLIAM BRECK,
Son of Robert Breck, Esq., and Mrs. Rachel Breck,
who departed this life September 11th, 1797,
in the 24th year of his age.

"Hark from the graves' oblivious doleful tones,
Here shall our names be mouldering like our bones,
Rise Immortal Soul, that hence my fame may shine,
Time flies and ends, eternity is thine."

In Memory of
Mr. JOSEPH HUNT BRECK,
who departed this life November 10th, A. D. 1801,
in the 36th year of his age.

"That life is long which answer's life's great end,
One eye on death and one full fixed on heaven,
Becomes a mortal and immortal man."

WILLIAM CLARK,
Died Dec. 31, 1842, Æ 78.

In Memory of
Mrs. JERUSHA CLARK,
wife of Mr. William Clark,
who died Feb. 7th, 1816, in the 52d year of her age.

Blessed are the dead who die in the Lord, for they rest from their labours and their works do follow them.

Mrs. MARY,
Wife of Mr. William Clark,
Died April 4, 1833, in the 70 year of her age.

In Memory of
Mr. LUCIUS CLARK,
who died Oct. 4, 1819, in the 31st year of his age.

All flesh is as grass and all the glory of man as the flower of grass. The grass withereth and the flower thereof falleth away.

In Memory of
Miss Miranda,
Daughter of William and Jerusha Clark,
who died Nov. 6, 1825, Æ 26 years.

"Rest thy hopes my friends on Christ the Lord,
Live while you live but to obey his word."

Also Sarah Clark,
of the same family, died in Sparta, N. J.,
Sept. 16, 1823, Æt 33 years.

John Moies,
Died Sept. 24, 1827, aged 50.

Mrs. Anna Moies,
Wife of Mr. John Moies,
died Aug. 1, 1823, aged 47 years.

In Memory of
Miss Elizabeth R. Moies,
who died May 30, 1818, in the 22 year of her age,
daughter of Mr. John and Mrs. Anna Moies.

Thus the bright damsel just reared her shining head,
From obscure shades of Life, and sunk among the dead.

Thomas Shepherd,
Born May 27, 1778, died Dec. 23, 1846.

Catherine,
his wife, born Dec. 23, 1782, died Nov. 24, 1846.

Elizabeth,
Wife of Henry Shepherd,
born Sept. 30, 1817, died Jan. 23, 1848.

Ogden E. Edwards,
Born 11 Nov. 1802, died 25 April, 1848.

EPITAPHS. 95

CATHERINE,
Daughter of T. Shepherd, Esq. of Northampton,
and wife of Ogden E. Edwards of New York,
born 1806, Aug. 22, died 1843, April 21,
aged 36 years and 8 months.
"An Angel's arm can't snatch us from the grave,
Legions of Angels can't confine us there."

MARY S.
died 1834, May 3,
age 1 year 10 months and 28 days.

THOMAS S.
died 1827, Dec. 10,
aged 1 year 3 months 9 days.

EUGENE,
died 1837, Dec. 10,
aged 1 year 2 months 12 days.

POMEROY,
an Infant, died 1843, March 11.
Children of Ogden E. Edwards and Catherine S.
Edwards of New York.

FENNER.

CHARLES P. KINGSLEY,
died June 2, 1844, aged 45.

CHARLES B.
son of Cha's. P. and Caroline Kingsley,
died Aug. 7, 1832, aged 11 mon.

EDWARD B.
son of L. H. and Nancy B. Graves,
died Sept. 6, 1844.

EPITAPHS.

Marie Louise,
daught. of George and H. A. Abbott, died
Nov. 10, 1846, aged 7 months.
Sweet babe, thy parents' loss is thy gain.

Mr. Timothy Graves,
Died Oct. 15, 1829, in the 40th year of his age.

Mrs. Experience,
wife of Justin Smith, died Jan. 16, 1832, aged 55 years.
"This mould'ring dust shall here repose in peace,
Till that great day when time itself shall cease;
Her Spirit is with God, and this its plea,
My Saviour died, my Saviour died for me."

James Clinton,
Son of Charles A. and Caroline H. Dewey,
Died Dec. 3, 1832, aged 7 years.

Edward J.,
Son of Charles A. and Caroline H. Dewey,
died May 4, 1836, aged 3 years and 6 months.

Henry C.,
Son of Charles A. and Caroline H. Dewey,
died April 18, 1836, aged 17 months.

In Memory of
Almira Granger,
Wife of Ebenezer Granger,
who died Oct. 5, 1825, aged 17.

In Memory of
Mr. Moses Parsons,
who died June 1, 1814,
in the 83 year of his age.
"Though I pass through this gloomy vale,
Where death and all its horrors are,
My heart and hope shall never fail,
For God my Shepherd's with me there."

CALEB STRONG,

Late Governor of Massachusetts.

In Memory of
CALEB STRONG,
late Governor of Massachusetts,
who, after a life universal for piety and
devotion to the public service,
died Nov. 7, 1819,
in the 75th year of his age.
"The memory of the just is blessed."

In Memory of
Mrs. SARAH STRONG,
the wife of Caleb Strong, and daughter of
the Rev. John Hooker,
who, having early devoted herself to the service of her
Redeemer, and through life exemplified the virtues
and graces of his religion, gently breathed out
her spirit, in humble reliance upon his power
and love, on the 12th day of Feb., 1817, in the
60th year of her age.

Though hope and trust
And patient resignation shone serene,
The Christian's pattern, and the friends' support,
Their work fulfilled, those graces have resigned
Their seat to perfect love and endless praise.

In Memory of
SARAH STRONG,
the daughter of Caleb and Sarah Strong,
who died Oct. 26, 1783.
aged 2 yrs and 3 mos.

In Memory of
EDWARD STRONG,
Son of Caleb Strong, and Sarah, his wife.
He was born July 2, 1790, and educated at Harvard
College: but his fair prospects of usefulness and distinction were closed by his death, May 6, 1813,
in the 23 year of his age.
Ah! quam dispar monumentum!

Here lies the body of
PHEBE STRONG,
the daughter of Caleb Strong, Esq.,
and Mrs. Sarah, his wife,
who died Sept. 10, 1799,
aged 4 years and 5 months.

Here lies the body of
PHILIP STRONG,
the son of Caleb Strong, Esq.,
and Sarah, his wife,
died Aug. 17, 1800, aged 1 year and 5 months.

In Memory of
JULIA A. STRONG,
Daughter of Caleb Strong, and Sarah, his wife,
whose life was employed in active benevolence, and who
died in full hope of a happy immortality,
October 1st, 1818, aged 25 years.

Sweet peace, and heavenly hope, and humble joy,
Divinely beamed on her enraptured soul,
And crowned her for the skies,

ELIZABETH C.,
Daughter of Lewis and Maria Strong,
died June 1, 1815, aged 3 years.

JULIA M.,
Daughter of Lewis and Maria Strong,
died Nov. 20, 1822, aged 2 years and 5 months.

In remembrance of
REV. CALEB STRONG,
Son of Lewis and Maria Strong,
for seven years Pastor of the American Presbyterian
Church at Montreal, who died in that city,
universally beloved and lamented,
January 4, 1847, aged 31 years.

EPITAPHS. 99

Maria C.,
Daughter of Lewis and Maria Strong,
died Aug. 28, 1836, aged 8 years.

In remembrance of
THEODORE STRONG,
Son of Lewis and Maria Strong,
who, having secured the affection, and awakened
the fondest hopes of a large circle of friends,
died August 31, 1848, aged 22 years.

And they shall be mine, saith the Lord, in that day when I make
up my jewels.

MARIA ELIZABETH MATSON,
died May 11, 1847, aged 1 month.

Sleep on, thou sweet one, sleep—so early gone !
To earth a child is lost, to heaven a cherub born.

In Memory of
JULIA AUGUSTA STRONG,
youngest daughter of Theodore and Martha Strong,
Born March 30, 1822, died Nov. 10, 1827,
aged 5 years and 7 months.

Ere sin could blight, or sorrow fade,
Death came with friendly care,
The opening bud to heaven conveyed,
And bade it blossom there.

In memory of
MARTHA ANN STRONG,
Daughter of Theodore and Martha Strong,
was born June 3, 1811, and died Aug. 17, 1831,
in the 21st year of her age.

SARAH H. STONG,
Born Sept. 13, 1817, died Aug. 26, 1840.

SYLVESTER CLARK,
died Nov. 9, 1841, aged 55 years.

Sacred to the memory of
SYLVIA CHURCH,
A Colored woman, who for many years lived in
the family of N. Storrs, died 12 April, 1822, Æ 66.
Very few possessed more good qualities than she did. She was
for many years a member of Mr. Williams' Church, and
we trust lived agreeable to her profession, and is
now inheriting the promises.

In memory of
SARAH GRAY, A " Colored Woman."
Erected by those who experienced her faithful services.
She died Oct. 7, 1831, aged 23.

SOLOMON STODDARD,*
born Nov. 29, 1800, died Nov. 11, 1847.
In him were united eminent Literary attainments, sound and discriminating judgment, unaffected modesty and devoted Christian Character. After being connected with various Literary institutions, he was for the last nine years of his life Professor of Languages, in Middlebury College.
* Graduated at Yale College in 1820.

BENJA,
" Our Dear little Baby."

" A Polish Exile."
A. A. TARNAVA MALCHEWSKI,
vel, Jakubowski,
Obt. 24 Ap. 1837, aged 21.
Erected by his pupils.

CHARLOTTE S.
wife of J. C. Tabor, of New Bedford, Mass.
died April 21, 1837, aged 28.
" Fare thee well."

JAMES BRIDGMAN,
one of the
PILGRIM FATHERS,
Came from England, 1640,
came to this town, 1654,
Died 1676.

SARAH,
his wife, died Aug. 31, 1668.

JAMES,
his son, died Jan. 14, 1756, 7 mos.

SALLY MARIA,
Daughter of Thomas and Sally Maria Bridgman,
Born in Greenville, South Carolina, Nov. 14, 1822,
Died in Columbus, Ohio, March 3, 1834.

"Hark, they whisper Angels say,
Sister Spirit come away."
"Now I See."

HENRY BRIDGMAN,
Born in Columbus, May 17, 1836,
Died Aug. 14, 1837,
and is there interred by the side of his sister, S. M. B.

"And Jesus took a little Child."

JOSEPH COOK BRIDGMAN,
Born May 19, 1827, Died Sept. 14, 1846.
"Now I See."

In Memory of
THOMAS BRIDGMAN,* ESQ.,
who died Oct. 14th, 1771, in ye 31st year of his age.

Time was like the I life possess'd,
And time shall be when you shall rest.

* A descendant of James, grad. at Harvard 1762; M. A. at Yale 1765, studied Law with Major Joseph Hawley.

In Memory of
Mr. Thomas Bridgman,
who died Oct. yᵉ 30, 1742. * * *

[*Masonic Emblems.*]
Sacred to the memory of
Mr. Thomas Bridgman,
who died Aug. 5th, 1799, in the 32d year of his age.
"Farewell vain world, I must be gone,
I have no home or stay in thee,
I'll take my staff and travel on,
Till I a better world can see."

In memory of
Mrs. Elizabeth Bridgman,
Relict of Mr. Thomas Bridgman,
who died May 25th, 1806, aged 36.
"Jesus can make a dying bed
Feel soft as downy pillows are,
While on his breast I lean my head
And breathe my life out sweetly there."

William Bridgman,	Betsey,
Son of Thomas Bridgman,	Dauʳ of Mr. Thomas and
died Sept. 28, 1802,	Mrs. Elizabeth Bridgman,
aged 3 years.	died Feb. 20, 1798,
	aged 11 months.

Also an Infant,
who died July 8th, 1798.

SETH WRIGHT'S
FAMILY TOMB.

Hezekiah,
Son of Seth and Sarah Wright,
Died Feb. 14, 1815, Æ XXXI. y'rs.

EPITAPHS. 103

Theodore,
Son of S. and S. W., died June 21, 1839, Æ LV. y'rs.

Seth Wright,
Died Dec. 20, 1828, Æ LXXIV. y'rs.

Eliza P.,
Dau^tr of David and Sarah Adams,
Died July 26, 1815, Æ 17 mo's.

David Adams,
Died June 2, 1821, Æ XXXVI. y'rs.

Mary Eliza,
Dau^tr of D. and S. Adams, died July 12, 1825,
Æ IX. y'rs.

An Infant Child
of Hon. Benjamin and Mary Barrett,
died July 19, 1827.

Georgiana,
Dau^fr of Theodore and Mary Wright, died ——.

David,
Son of D. and S. Adams, died at Pittsfield,
Jan'y 10, 1835, Æ XIV. y'rs.

Sarah P.,
Dau^tr of D. and S. Adams, died Nov. 20, 1837,
Æ 19 y'rs.

Mary C.,
Dau^tr of Dr. James and Caroline Thompson,
Died May 24, 1846, Æ 17 mo's.

Sarah,
Wife of Seth Wright, died Aug. 26, 1846.
Æ LXXXVII. y'rs and XI. months.

Rebecca,
Sister of Hon. B. Barrett, died Oct. 3, 1846, Æ LX.

IN MEMORY OF
ISAAC CHAPMAN BATES,
WHO WAS BORN
AT GRANVILLE, MASS.,
JAN. 28, 1776, AND
DIED AT WASHINGTON, D. C.,
A SENATOR OF THE UNITED STATES,
MARCH 16, 1845.

Honored, Loved, Lamented. The Righteous hath hope in his Death.

GENERAL WILLIAM LYMAN,
American Consul at London,
Died September 2, 1811, in the 56th year of his age, at Cheltham, England, and was interred in Gloucester Cathedral.

In memory of
Mrs. CLARISSA WALDO,
Died Aug. 22, 1820, aged 58.
"Blessed are the dead who die in the Lord."

HUNTINGTON.

HELEN BETHIAH H.
daughter of C. P. H. & H. S. H.
died July 25, 1839.

HELEN SOPHIA,
wife of C. P. H.
eldest daughter of Hon. E. H. Mills,
died March 30, 1844.

HENRIETTE MILLS H.
Infant Child,
Feb^y, 8, 1844.

HANNAH DRAYTON,
of Charleston, South Carolina,
Ob. 12 April, 1833, Æ 60.

HARRIET,
daughter of Thomas and Harriet Edwards,
died March 4, 1833, aged 7 months and four days.

"None are too pretty, none too young,
To go to God, from whom they sprung."

In Memory of
Mr. HOLISTER BAKER,
who died Nov. 12, 1811,
in the 62 year of his age.

" Well, the kind minute must appear,
When we shall leave these bodies here,
These clogs of clay, and mount on high,
To join the songs above the sky."

In Memory of
Mr. NATHANIEL LUDDEN,
who died Nov. 22, 1814, aged 28 years.

Friends and physicians could not save,
This mortal body from the grave.
When Christ commands, it must appear.
* * * *

SARAH,
Wife of John Wright, died May 20, 1842,
aged 58.

In memory of
Mr. SAMUEL WRIGHT,
who died June 23, 1818, aged 66 years.

Mrs. JERUSHA LYMAN,
Wife of General William Lyman,
departed this life June 11, 1803,
in the 43d year of her age.

FROM ANCIENT RECORDS OF NONOTUCK.

The Grants of each mans to full sum of Acres of Land wch were Given to each Perticular Person, to be to them And to their heirs Execut's Assignes, to have And to hold forever feburary 19 : 1660.

Acres beside homelots.		Acres beside homelots.	
Roberd Bartlet,	57	Joseph Fitch,	60
Edward Elmore,	72	John Broughton,	27
William Elmore,	86	Thomas Bascom,	32
Richard Limon,	81	Roberd Limon,	32
John Limon,	53	James Bridgman,	38
Thomas Mason,	—	Gorge Langton,	38
Thomas Root,	51	John Ingersole,	23
William Janes,	34	Joseph Root,	10
Alexander Edwards,	72	Joseph Janes, 8, 3 Rood,	08
John Web,	37	Authur Williams,	20
Sam'l Wright, Sen'r,	54	John Stebings,	—
Samuel Wright, Jr.,	38	Roberd hanerd,	20
William hubberd,	43	John Pinchon,	120
Nathaniel Phelps,	29	Mr. Eleazer Mather,	41
William Miller,	45	Edward Baker,	22
David Bvrt,	39	William Clark,	86
Walter Lee,	19	Hinry Woodward,	46
Thomas Woodford,	33	Hinry Cundlief,	20
Isack Shelden,	31	Enos Kingsley,	06
John King,	26	Gorge Sumner,	08
Samvel Allyn,	26	Ralph Hutchinton,	06
Thomas Salmon,	22	William Smeed,	06
Christopher Smith,	17	Aaron Cook, Senr,	—
Hinry Curtis,	34	David Wilton,	—
William Hannum,	25	John Strong,	—
John Hannum,	15	Medad Pumry,	16
Gorge Alexander,	32½	Jonathan Hunt,	16
John Blisse,	21	Joshua Carter,	10
Joseph Persons,	81	Mr. James Cornish,	—

Here foloweth a coppei of the writing that is in Mr. Mather's hands About peticular mens Lands wch were given to Mr. Mather to dispose of for the common good of the towne of Northampton.

Theese pesants witneseth that we whose Names are under subscribed doe promise and ingage to part with such summs of Land to which our Names Are Anexed upon the Consideration that Mr.

EPITAPHS.

Mather, *non Resident* Amongst us shall have the disposing of sd Lands to such inhabitants as the sd Mather shall Judge behovefull and needfull for the well being of the towne of Northampton, to be devided Acording to ye same rule by which we devided the Lands ourselves, have or shall have in possession that is to say 20 Acres to 100lb and 15 Acres to A person, and All the Lands we Abate or part with all shall be laid together as the —— end of the meadow we commonly call Manhan.

Samuel Wright, Junr.,	04	John Stebings,	02
William Holton,	10	Isack Shellden,	06
Joseph Fitch,	19	Thomas Salmon,	02
Joseph Persons,	08	Roberd hanerd,	03
Richard Limon,	09	Thomas Woodford,	06
John Limon,	05	John Ingersole,	03
Thomas Root,	05	William Miller,	06
Thomas Mason and Samuel Allyn,	10	Walter Lee,	03
		William Hannum,	03
William Hubberd,	05	John Hannum,	01
William Janes,	04	Thomas Bascom,	04
Allexander Edwards,	05	Hinry Curtice,	05
Roberd Bartlet,	05	James Bridgman,	04
Nathaniel Phelps,	03	Roberd Limon,	03
Authur Williams,	05	John Blisse,	02
John King,	03	Gorge Allexander,	03
John Broughton,	03	Christouer Smith,	03
Samuell wright, Junr,	03	Gorge Langton,	04
David Burt,	03		

A COPY OF THE ORIGINAL DEED FROM THE INDIANS OF NORTHAMPTON.

Be It known by these presents, That CRIKWOLLOP (alias) WAHILLOWA, NENESHALANT, NASSICOHEE, KIUNKS, PAQUAHALANT, ASSELLAQUOMPAS, and ANOWUSK, the wife of WALLUTHER, All of Nonotuck, who are the chief and proper owners of all the lands on the west side of Connecticut River, at Nonotuck, on the one, Do give, grant, bargain, and sell unto JOHN PYNCHON, of Springfield, on the other part, To him, his heirs and assigns, All the grounds and meadows, woods and ponds and w*** lying on the west side of Quonecticutt River, Beginning the small River below MANHAN, called SANKROHONK, and so up by Quonetcutt River, to the little meadow called CAPAWONK, namely, to the little brook or gutter on this side CAPAWONK, which little brook is called MASQUANOPE, and the grounds lying westward from Connecticut River, within the compass aforesaid, for nine miles out in the woods (viz.) as far as MANSHOONISK, is from Springfield, (for so it was expressed to the Indians.) All that tract of ground from SANKRONK River, and QUONACKUCK called MANHAN, POIKNACK, PETOWAG, ASPOW-OUNK, LUCKCOMMUCK, ASSATAYYAGG, NAYYAGG, NANYGROMKEGG, MASGUMP, and by what other names the said grounds are called and all out into the wood from the great River for nine miles within the compass.

The aforesaid Indians, an particular, WAWHILLOWA, FENASSAHALANT, NASSACHOKEE, being the Sachems of Nonotuck, do for themselves and with the consent of the other Indians, and owners of the said grounds, sell, give, and grant unto JOHN PYNCHON, of Springfield, and to his assigns for and in the consideration of One Hundred fathoms of wampum by tale, and for ten coats, (besides some small gifts on hand paid to the said Sachems and owners all the land aforesaid, as these presents have bargained granted and sold to the said PYNCHON, all and singular the said lands, free from all incumbrances of Indians provided the said PYNCHON, shall plow up or caused to be plowed up, for the said Indians, Sixteen acres of land on the easterly side of QUONECTICUTT River which is to be done sometime next Summer, and in the mean (viz.) the next Spring 1654, the Indians have liberty to plant their present cornfields, but after that time, they are wholly to leave the west side of the River and not to plant or molest the English there. All the same premises, the said PYNCHON, and his assigns shall have and enjoy absolutely and clearly forever, all incumbrances from any Indians or their cornfields.

In Witness of these presents the said Indians have subscribed their marks this Twenty-fourth day of September, 1653,

    The mark of ⋈ CRIKWALLOP,
    " " " ⋈ NENESSAHALNNT,
    " " " ⋈ NASSICOHEE,
    " " " ⋈ PAQUAHALANT,

The underwriten are witnesses that these are the marks of the Sachems, within mentioned and that they do freely pass over the land within mentioned in the behalf of themselves and other owners to JOHN PYNCHON, of Springfield, and to his assigns forever.

ELIZUR HOLYOKE, The mark ⋈ of WATCHANINE,
HENRY BURT, A Chief man who helped to make the bargain,
THOMAS COOPER, The mark ⋈ of NAMSNELECK,
THOMAS STEBBINS, The mark ⋈ SKITTOMP, (alias) UNQUASK.

SPRINGFIELD

"Take them O Death! and bear away
Whatever thou can'st call'thine own!
Thine image stamped upon this clay,
Doth give thee that, but that alone!

"Take them, O Grave! and let them lie
Folded upon thy narrow shelves,
As garments by the soul laid by,
And precious only to ourselves!

"Take them, O great Eternity!
Our little life is but a gust,
That bends the branches of thy tree,
And trails its blossoms in the dust!"
LONGFELLOW.

HERE LyE^TH THE BoDy oF
MARi
THE WIFE oF ELIZVR HoLyoKE
WHo DIED OCToBER 26 1657.

Shee yt lyes here was while shee stood
A very Glory of Woomanhood
Even here was Sowne most PRETious DVST
Which Surely Shall Rise wiTH The JusT.

Here lyeth the Body of
JOHN GLOVER
Son of MR PelATIAH Glover
who Died y^E 14 oF IANVARy 1664.

My Body Sleeps my SoVLE HATH SVIET REST
in ARMES oF GoD in Christ who makes me Blest
The Tyme Drawes on apace when GoD yE Sonne
To See his face shall both VNITE In oNE.

AbILENE HA
WIFE oF M^R JAP
CHAPI^N Dy^D oN No^R
y^E 17 1711 AGE^D 68
yEAR.

MR
JAPHAT CHAPIN
Dy^D oN FEb^R y^E 20
1712 AGE^D 70 yEAR.

LIEV^N
AbEL WRIGHT Dy^D
IN OCT^R y^E 29 AN
NO^D 1725 AGE^D———94 yEAR^S.

SARAH
y^E WIFE of DAVID CHAPIN
DyE^D oN FEb^R y^E 6 1725-^{6}
AGE^D 38 yEA^R.

Wid. MARGARET BLISS
Settled in this town 1645,
Died April 28, 1684.
SAMUEL,
Her son, died March 23, 1720.
EBENEZER,
His son, died Sept. 7, 1717.
JEDEDIAH,
First son, died Nov. 30, 1777, Æ 69.
RACHEL,
His wife, died Nov. 10, 1747.
MARIAM,
His 2d wife, died Nov. 19, 1793.
ALEX BLISS,
Died July 25, 1843, Æ 90.

MARGARET,
His wife, died March 21, 1788, Æ 29.
ABIGAL,
His 2d wife, died July 6, 1807, Æ 39.
Their Children.
EDMUND BLISS, Esq.
Died April 16, 1821, Æ 35.
ALEX BLISS, Esq.
Died at Plymouth, July 15, 1827, Æ 35.
MARGARET
Died April 27, 1790, Æ 2 ys.
THOMAS W.
Died August, 1799, Æ 8 ys.
RICHARD
Died Sept. 13, 1807, Æ 10 days.
THOMAS W.
Died May 7, 1802, Æ 8 mos.

EDMUND
Died Feb. 28, 1823, Æ 17 ms.
ELIJAH
Died July 24, 1831, Æ 4 ys.
Children of Elijah W. and Orphana Bliss.
Also 10 children who died under 3 ys of age.

In Memory of
ye Hon. JOHN PYNCHON, Esq.
who died Jan^{ry} 17th, 1702-3,
aged 76 years.
Also Mrs. AMY,
his wife died Jan^{ry} 9th, 1698-9,
aged 74 years.
Also WILLIAM,
their son, died June 15th, 1654,
aged 1 year.

Also MAHITABLE,
their Dau^tr, died July 24th, 1663,
aged 2 years.
Also of Hon. JOHN PYNCHON, Esq.
died April 25th, 1721, aged 74 years.
Also Mrs. MARGARET,
his wife, died Nov^br 11th, 1716,
aged —— years.
Also JOHN PYNCHON 3d, Esq.
died July 12th, 1742,
aged 68 years.
Also Mrs. BATHSHUA,
his 1st wife, died June 20th, 1710,
aged 27 years.
Also Mrs. PHEBE,
his 2d wife, died Oct^br 10th, 1722,
aged 36.
Also Mr. JOHN PYNCHON,
his son, died April 6th, 1754,
aged 49 years.
Also WILLIAM PYNCHON, Esq.
Son of ye Hon. John Pynchon 2d, Esq.
died Jan^ry 1st, 1741,
aged 52 years.
Also Mrs. KATHERINE,
his wife died April 10th, 1747,
aged 47 years.
Also Mrs. SARAH,
their Dau^tr, wife of Josiah Dwight Esq.
died Aug^st 4th, 1755,
aged 34 years.
Hon JOSEPH PYNCHON,
Died 1765.
EDWARD PYNCHON Esq.
Died Nov. 3, 1777, Æ 63.

WILLIAM PYNCHON, Esq.,
Son of John Pynchon 3d, died Jan. 11, 1783,
Æ 80.

SARAH,
Relict of Wm. Pynchon, Esq.
Died Feb. 21, 1776,
Æ 84.

ELIZABETH,
Relict of Benj. Colton,
Daughter of John Pynchon, 3d, Esq.
Died Sept. 26, 1776, Æ 74.

Cap. GEORGE PYNCHON,
Son of John Pynchon 3d, died June 26, 1797,
aged 81.

Maj. WM. PYNCHON,
Died Mar. 24, 1808, aged 60.

LUCY,
His wife, died Feb. 17, 1814,
aged 75.

JOHN PYNCHON,
Died Mar. 4th, 1826, aged 84.

EDWARD PYNCHON Esq.,
Died March 17, 1830, aged 56 years.

WM. PYNCHON,
Died Aug. 12, 1847, aged 71 years.

NOTE.—He lived in the "OLD PYNCHON HOUSE" 19 years.
It was torn down in 1831, having stood 171 years.

This Monument is erected
to the memory of
Col. WILLIAM SMITH,
who departed this life Feby. 17, 1806,
aged 50 years.

I know that my redeemer liveth, and that he shall stand at the latter day upon the earth and though after my skin, worms destroy this body yet in my flesh shall I see God.

This Monument is erected
to the memory of
Mrs. Sophia Byers,
Consort of Mr. James Byers, Jun.
born Sept. 4th, 1776,
died February 23d, 1803,
aged 26 years.

"The bliss of human kind fleets fast away
From dreams of hope, alas! how soon were torn,
The sun of joy scarce darts its gladning ray,
When clouds o'ershadow and we wake to mourn.

This Monument is erected
to the memory of
Capt. James Byers,
who departed this life
the 2d day of Nov. 1811,
Æt 70 years.

This Monument is erected
in memory of
Mrs. Hannah Byers,
relict of the late
James Byers, Esq.
who died Oct. 10th, 1815,
aged 68 years.

In Memory of
John Bryant,
born in Boston 11th May, 1743,
died in this town 1st May, 1816,
aged 73.

Also of his wife,
Hannah Mason Bryant,
Born in Boston, Dec. 21, 1757,
Died in this town, Dec. 21, 1829.

Here rests the remains of
HENRY KNOX BRYANT,
Son of Capt. John and Mrs. Hannah Bryant,
who died 2d Dec. 1792,
in the 3^d year of his age.

Here rests the remains of
CAPT. DAVID MASON,
who died Feb^r 8th, 1795,
aged 42.
"A Law Eternal has decreed,
That all things born shall mortal be."

Gen. JACOB BLISS,
Died March 27, 1829, Æ 66.

Col. JOHN BLISS,
Died Dec. 24, 1827, Æ 37.

JACOB BLISS, Jun.,
Died at New Orleans, Oct. 14, 1819,
Æ 24.

In Memory of
EMILY,
Daughter of Jacob and Mary Bliss,
Born Dec. 2d, 1798,
Died Aug. 13th, 1800,
Æ 29 months.

Here lies intered the body of
LIEUT. TIMOTHY BLISS,
who died Augst ye 18th A. D. 1769,
in ye 57th year of his age.
"Hark from the tombs a doleful sound,
Mine ears attend the cry,
Ye living men come view the ground,
Where you must shortly lie."

Here lies intered the body of
Mr. JOHN MALLEFUILD,
A French gentleman, who, passing through the town of Springfield, dying, bequeathed all his estate to the poor of this town.
He died Nov. 26, 1711.
Psal. 41, 1. Blessed is he that considereth the poor.

In Memory of the
Rev. ROBERT BRECK, A. M.,
late pastor of the church of Christ in this place,
who died on the 23^d, day of April,
A. D. 1784,
in the 71st year of his age,
and in the 49th, of his ministry.

This monument is erected by his affectionate and grateful parishioners, in addition to that in their breasts, to perpetuate the remembrance of his singular worth and long continued labors among them in the service of their souls.
He taught us how to live, and Oh! too high
A price for knowledge! taught us how to die.

Heare Liys the Body of
BENIAMIN WRIGHT,
He deceased the 24th of October,
1704, at near the age of 78 years.

Here lies ye Body of
MARY SIKES, once
Mary Warner, Died March 13, 1724.

In Memory of
Ensign INCREASE SIKES,
who died March 13th, 1760,
in his 59th year.

Here lies ye body of
MARY SIKES,
once Mary Knolton, who dyed ye 1 of ianvary 1707^8
aged 30 years.

In Memory of
Doc^{tr} JONATHAN BLISS,
whose Body was weak, His mind Strong,
His heart upright, and his life exemplary,
He died Oct. 29th, 1761, in his 63d year,
and here lies intered.

In Memory of
Doct. PELATIAH BLISS,
who being abroad in the Public Service,
as Surgeon of a Regiment,
Died near Albany, Decr 26, 1756,
in his 34th year.

Also in Memory of
PELATIAH,
his Son, who died Novr 8th, 1766,
in his 18th year, and was here intered,
of Suffield.

Here lies intered the body of
the Rev^d Mr. DAN^{EL} BREWER,
the late worthy Pastor of the first Church in Springfield,
who departed this life on the 5th of Novem^{br} 1733,
in the 66th year of his age, and
40th of his Ministry.

Rev. 14th, 13th. Blessed are the dead that die in the Lord, they rest from their labours, and their works follow them.

Here lies intered the body of
Mr. DANIEL BREWER, JUN^R
who dec^d October ye 7th, 1733,
in the 25th year of his age.

He was an hard Student, a Great Scholar, and a good Christian. He esteem'd the Riches and Glory of this world as loss and Dung, so that He might win Christ, Having a desire to depart. He lived much desir'd, and Dy'd Greatly Lamented.

In Memory of
Mrs. KATHERINE,
late wife of y° Reverend Mr. Daniel Brewer,
who died May 15th, 1754,
in her 79th year.

In Memory of
NATHANIEL BREWER,
Died March 11, 1796, aged 85.
Also of EUNICE, his wife,
Died Dec. 28th, 1774, aged 66.
Also Doct. CHAUNCY BREWER,
Died March 15, 1830, aged 87.
Also of AMY, his wife,
Died May 21, 1821, aged 76.
Also of LUCY, their daughter,
Died March 19th, 1801, aged 29.
And of KATE, their daughter,
Died Nov. 9th, 1786, aged 2 years.

In Memory of
Mr. CHARLES BREWER,
who died 12th Mar^h, 1793, aged 76.
Depart my friends, dry up your tears,
I must lie here till Christ appears.

In Memory of
Mrs. ANNE BREWER,
Relict of Mr. Charles Brewer,
who died March 24, 1798, aged 86 years.

SUSAN FREEDOM,
Died Dec. 28th, 1803, aged 19.

Tho' short her life, and humble her station, she faithfully performed all the duties of it. "The wise and great could do no more."

NOTE.—(A Colored Girl,) bro't up by Col. Worthington.

EPITAPHS.

In Memory of
JOHN HUGGINS,
G E N T L E M A N,
who died August 1st, 1732,
aged —— years.

In Memory of 2 sons of
Mr. ELLIS RUSSELL,
who were both drowned together May 23, 1783,
viz. Mr. STEPHEN RUSSELL, in ye 31 year of his age,
and ARCHELAUS, in ye 13 year of his age.
Reader beware, and venture not too far,
To save one drowning, lest my fate you share.
The second I ventured in to save,
A brother drowning, brought me to my grave.

In Memory of
Mrs. ABIGAL,
wife of Mr. Jacob Cooley,
who died Jan^{ry} 12th, 1786,
aged 63 years.
Be meek and lowly O my friends,
Behold this lonesome tomb,
Beside of me there is a place,
Prepare to enter down.

Here rests the body of
LUKE HITCHCOCK, Esq.
who after he had serv^d God and his generation in
several publick offices, deceased Jany 24th, 1727,
in ye 72d year of his age.

| HOOKER. |
| 'Rest in Hope.' |

JOHN HOOKER,
Died Mar. 7, 1829, Æ 69.
SARAH,
his wife, died Sept. 5, 1842, aged 78.

Two children died in infancy.
RICHARD,
April 24, 1802, aged 9 mo.
CLARRISA,
Oct. 8, 1804, aged 8 mo.
MARY,
Died July 17, 1824, aged 25.
SARAH,
wife of Dr. Hale, died April 21, 1825, aged 30.
ALMIRA,
Her only child, died Oct. 15, 1824, aged 6 mo.

SARAH DWIGHT,
Daughter of George and Rachel Hooker,
Died April 18, 1824, aged 5 ys. and 3 mo.

In Memory of
LUCY ASHMUN,
Daut^r of George and Rachel Hooker,
who died Oct. 1, 1823, aged 9 months.

JOHN HOOKER,
Eldest child of F. A. & E. D. Packard,
Born Jan. 20, 1827,
Died Jan. 20, 1829.

The flower fadeth, but the word of * * * *

OSGOOD.

HENRY
Died July 3, 1834, aged 3 years.
MARY SHERBURNE,
Died June 19, 1843, aged 29 years.

In Memory of
Mr. Earl Cooley,
who by a casual blow in a well, died 15th Nov. 1809,
in the 50th year of his age.

Susan Sanborn,
Wife of Simon Sanborn,
Died May 3, 1834.

In Memory of
Mr. Johnathan Lyman,

Born in Lebanon, educated in Yale College where he 5 years acceptably and worthily discharged the duties of a tutor, the last winter was an instructor in the academic school at Hatfield, and for 2 years past a preacher universally approved. Returning from Hatfield, on a visit to his parents he was taken sick in this town, and after 3 days, on May 4th, 1766, in the 29th year of his age, he breathed his immortal soul into the hands of Jesus. His body lies buried here, waiting for a happy Resurrection.

In Memory of the
Hon. Thomas Dwight,
who died Jan. 2^d,
A. D. 1819, aged 60.

Behold he taketh away who can hinder him? who will say unto him what doest thou?

Mrs. Hannah Dwight,
Relict of Thomas Dwight,
Died July 10, 1833,
Æ 73.

Sacred to the Memory of
Hon. Jonathan Dwight,
who was born in this town Dec. 28, 1772,
and died March 22, 1840,
VIRTUTE, VIXIT, MEMORIA,
VIVIT.

In Memory of
Miss Margaret Dwight,
who Died
April 24th, MDCCXC,
in the 20th, year of her age.
This Monument is erected.

Why are friends ravish'd from us, 'tis to bind
By soft affections ties on human hearts,
The thought of death which reason too supine,
Or misemployed, so rarely fasten there.

James Scutt Dwight,
Died March 18, 1822,
aged 53.
Mary Sandford,
wife of James Scutt Dwight,
Died Dec. 7, 1844,
aged 70.

James S. Dwight,
Son of James Scutt Dwight,
Died at Florence, Italy,
Feb. 24, 1831,
aged 33.

Jonathan Dwight,
Died Sep. 5, 1831,
Æ 88.

In Memory of
Mrs. Hannah Dwight,
Consort of Jonathan Dwight, Esq.
who died
May XXVI, MDCCCXXIV,
aged LXXIX.

The days of our years are threescore years and ten, and if by reason of strength they be fourscore years, yet is their strength, labor and sorrow, for it is soon cut off and we fly away.

Sacred to the Memory of
Mr. ROYAL BOND,
Merchant
of New York,
formerly of Boston,
who was drowned on the
night of the 10th, August, 1815,
in attempting to cross the ferry at this place,
aged 28 years.

The way of man is not in himself. It is not in man that walketh to direct his steps.

CYRUS POMEROY,
Son of Cyrus and Miranda Cole,
Died July 30, 1847,
Æ 17 Months, and 12 days.

CHILD.

ANN,
wife of William Child,
Died April 26, 1846,
Æ 58.

WILLIAM CHILD, Esq.
Died June 27, 1847,
Æ 59.

MARTHA COGGESHALL,
Daughter of
G. W. and Isabella Callender,
Died June 14, 1839,
Æ 2 years and 8 Months.

'Tho' lost to sight, in memory dear.'

JOHN PHELPS,
son of
Harvey, and Hannah Chapin,
Died Aug. 25, 1826,
Æ 7 Months.

ERASTUS S. CHAPIN,
Died May 1st 1840,
Æ 21 years.

Now let our mourning hearts revive,
And all our tears be dry,
Why should these eyes be drown'd in grief
Which view a Saviour nigh.

In Memory of
FRANCIS NEWTON,
Son of Erastus and Ulrica Chapin,
who was drowned Aug. 5th, 1820,
aged 7 years 10 mo. and 9 days.

Boast not thyself of to-morrow, for thou knowest not what a
day may bring forth.

Dr. SAM¹ KINGSBURY,
Died June 18, 1826, aged 46.

JEMIMA,
His wife, died Jan. 20, 1846,
Æ 62.

CHARLES L.,
their Son, died March 23, 1843,
Æ 34.

WARE.
WILLIAM H. WARE,
Died Sept. 17, 1840, Æ 2 yrs, and 4 mo.

MARY ELIZA,
wife of Addison Ware, died April 14, 1846,
Æ 38.

EPITAPHS.

In Memory of
Ensign JAMES WARRINER,
who, after an useful and exemplary life,
died May 9th, 1765,
in yᵉ 73d year of his age.
To ye great grief of his friends.

Here lies the body of
MARTHA WARRINER,
who died Sept. 23d, 1744,
in yᵉ 27 year of her age.

Here lyeth the body of
Lievᵗ JAMES WARRINER,
who died March 17, in the
68 year of his age, 1736.

Here lyeth the body of
Mr. THOMAS WARRINER,
Son of Lieut. James Warriner,
and his wife, who died June the 13th,
in the 37th year of his age,
ANO 1740.

Here lyeth the body of
Ensign EBENEZER WARRINER,
who died on the fifth day of February,
in the fifty-fifth year of his age, 1737.

In Memory of
ARABILLA,
Daughter of Mr. Judah Chapin and Mrs. Lois Chapin,
who died August 24th, 1798,
aged 2 years and 8 months.

"The dear delight we here enjoy,
And fondly call our own,
Are but short favors borrowed now,
To be repaid anon."

11*

In Memory of
Mrs. JOANNA,
wife of Mr. Samuel Brooks,
who died March 17, 1756,
in her 45th year.

In Memory of
Capt. JAMES SCUTT,
who died Sept. ye 10th, A. D. 1769,
in ye 87th year of his age.

In Memory of
Mrs. ELIZABETH SCUTT,
wife of Capt. James Scutt, who died May 21st, A. D. 1770,
in the 82d year of her age.

Mrs. EUNICE BRECK,
the Virtuous Consort of the
Rev^d. ROBERT BRECK,
and Daughter of the
Rev^d. DANIEL BREWER,
was born May 28th, A. D. 1707,
and died Augst. 12th, A. D. 1767,
and lies here Intered.

Oh! could we die with those yt die,
And place us in their stead;
Then would our Spirits learn to fly,
And convers with the Dead.

THOMAS SARGEANT,
Died May 16th, 1834,
aged 61 years.

THOMAS SARGEANT, Jr.
Died at sea June 25th, 1825,
aged 27 years.

EPITAPHS. 127

ELLEN SARGEANT,
Daughter of Henry and Mary M. Sargeant,
Died Feb. 27th, 1836,
aged 2 years.

MARY SARGEANT,
Daughter of Henry and Mary M. Sargeant,
Died Nov. 2d, 1838,
aged 7 years.

EDWARDS.

ELISHA EDWARDS,
Died Feb. 7th, 1840,
aged XLV.

FRANK EDWARDS,
Born April 20th 1824,
Died Oct. 24, 1825.

An Infant son,
Born Dec. 21, 1831,
Died Jan. 22, 1832.

STANLEY EDWARDS,
Born Nov. 26, 1838,
Died May 23, 1839.

In Memory of
Mrs. SIBYL BONTECOU,
Wife of Daniel Bontecou,
who died May 5th, 1810,
in the 29th year of her age.
My days are past, my purposes are broken off.

WILLIAMS.

Eleazer Williams,
Died Oct. 3, 1834.
Æ 64.

Mrs. Charlotte Williams,
Died Feb. 22, 1827,
Æ 54.

W. DWIGHT.

Thomas, Oct. 5, 1840.
" Sept. 1, 1841.

Ann M.
Died June 10, 1844,
Æ 2 weeks.

Susan A.
Died Nov. 24, 1844,
Æ 6 mo.
Twin Daughters of Josiah and Maria D. Hunt.

In Memory of
Sarah H. Bancroft,
wife of George Bancroft, Esq.,
Born Jan. 22, 1803, died June 26, 1837.

Mary Cushing,
Daughter of Geo. and Martha E. Ashmun,
Born April 2, 1835, died Oct. 9, 1838.

Sarah Haviland,
Daughter of Geo. and Martha E. Ashmun,
Born March 19, 1837, died May 28, 1838.

WILLIAM AUGUSTUS,
Son of Hon. Charles Stearns,
Born Feb. 7, 1843, died Oct. 3, 1845.

Sacred to the Memory of
SARAH,
Widow of Hon. Jonathan Dwight,
who died Dec. 24, 1848,
aged 73.
"Her children arise up and call her blessed."

MRS. CAROLINE,
Wife of Oliver B. Morris,
and daughter of the late Hon. George Bliss, Esq.,
Died Feb. 9th, 1842, aged 50.

HENRY O.
Son of Henry and Mary Morris,
Died May 3, 1845, Æ 10 mo.

Mrs. ELIZABETH,
Wife of Elam Stockbridge,
Died Oct. 20, 1826, Æ 49.

DOROTHY A.
Daughter of Elam and Elizabeth Stockbridge,
Died Feb. 11, 1838, aged 20.

FREDERICK BRYANT,
Died Jan. 21, 1832, Æ 4 ms.

FREDERICK BRYANT,
Died June 9th, 1839.

In Memory of
Mr. JAMES B. SMITH,
who died in France, Dec. 13, A. D. 1821, aged 34.
Absent or dead, still let a friend be dear,
A sigh the absent claim, the dead a tear.

ADONIJAH FOOT,
Born Oct. 22, 1780, died Oct. 13, 1825,
Æ 45.

ADONIJAH,
Son of Adonijah and Clarissa Foot,
Died March 12, 1823, Æ 3.

FESTUS STEBBINS,
Died June 21, 1850, aged 82.

In Memory of
MOSES BLISS, ESQ.,
Many years a Judge of the Court of Common Pleas,
and Deacon of the Church.
He died July 4th, 1814, in the 79th year of his age.

In Memory of
Mrs. ABIGAL BLISS,
Consort of Moses Bliss, Esq.,
who died Aug. 29, 1800,
in the 63d year of her age.

ZEBINA STEBBINS,
Died Oct. 6, 1835, aged 80.

THOMAS STEBBINS,
Died March 1, 1836, aged 79.

NOTE.—John Dwyt, or Dwite, or Dwight, supposed to be the root of all of that name in America, came to this country in 1636. He was the son of a wool-comber. He settled in Dedham. His eldest son, Richard, was lost in the wilderness, when about seven years old. Timothy, his only remaining son, married Reua Flint, by whom he had ten children. Henry, the fourth surviving son of Timothy, married and settled in Hatfield, died 1732. His son, Josiah, settled in Springfield, and died 1768. His son, Edmund, removed to Halifax, and died 1755. Josiah was the father of Thomas Dwight, and Edmund of Jonathan Dwight of this town.

HADLEY.

"Where are the flowers, the fair young flowers, that lately sprung and stood,
In brighter light and softer airs, a beauteous sisterhood?
Alas! they all are in their graves, the gentle race of flowers
Are lying in their lowly beds, with the fair and good of ours;
The rain is falling where they lie; but the cold November rain
Calls not from out the gloomy earth the lovely one again —W. C. Bryant.

[The oldest Monument.]
DOC^r IOHN WESTGARR^e DyED
IN SEP^r 1675 IN y^e
XXXI yEAR oFs AGE.

EN^s
CHILEAb SMITH DyE^d oN
MARCH ye 7, 1731 AGE^d
96 yEAR AND HANNAH HIS
WIFE DyE^d oN AVGst 31 1733
AGE^d 88 yEARS.
IT^s WoRTHY oF MEMoRI^L y^t THEY
LIVE^d IN MARiAG STA^t 70 yEAR.

REBEKAH MADE
BY GOD A MEIT HELP
To MR JOHN RVSSELL
AND FELLOW LABOVRER IN
CHRISTS WORK
A WISE VERTVOVS PiOVS MOTHER
IN ISRAEL LyES HERE
IN FVLL ASSVRANCE oF A IoYFVL
RESVRRECTION
SHE DIED IN
THE 57 yEAR oF
HER AGE NOVEMB^r 21
1 6 8 8

EPITAPHS.

```
33 yEARS FAITHFVLLY GOVERND   REVEREND  RVS           SELLS REMAINS WHO FIRST GAT
                               THE  FLOCK  OF
                            CHRIST  IN  HADLEY
                               TIL  THE  CHIEF
                            SHEPHERD  SVDEN
                            LLy  BVT  MERCIFV
                            LLy  CALLᵈ  HIM  oFF
                            TO  RECEIEV  HIS  REW
                               ARD  IN  THE  66
                               yEAR  oF  HIS  AGE
                               DECEMBER  10
                                    1692
                               HERD  AND  FOR
```

GOFFE and WHALLEY, two of the judges of Charles I. were concealed from the rage of their pursuers for several years, in the Rev. Mr. Russell's cellar. One of them was there for a long time, and was so carefully screened from the public eye, that none of Mr. Russell's neighbors had any knowledge of the circumstance.

The tradition is that on a certain occasion, when the town was beset by Indians, an aged man of a remarkably venerable aspect with a long beard, white as the driven snow, suddenly rushed into the engagement, fought with wonderful adroitness, animated the soldiers by his cheering language and valiant conduct, and after repelling the enemy, immediately withdrew to his place of concealment. It was reported that an angel had appeared with a sword, and achieved the victory.

Sacred to the Memory of
Capⁿ. MOSES PORTER,
who was born at Hadley,
Jan. 13ᵗʰ, A. D. 1721,
and was slain by the Indians
near Crown Point, in the morning scout
of the 8ᵗʰ, of Sep. 1755.
" Earths highest station ends in here he lies,
" But life immortal waits beyond the grave."

EPITAPHS. 133

This Stone is erected to the
Memory of Miss MARY KELLOGG,
only daugher of Doct. Giles C. Kellogg,
who died Nov. 11, 1802,
in the 18th year of her age.

[Lines written by President Dwight, in whose family Miss K.
had been an inmate.]

Stay, thoughtful mourner, hither led
To weep, and mingle with the dead ;
Pity the maid, who slumbers here,
And pay the tributary tear.—
Thy feet must wander far to find
A fairer form, a lovelier mind ;
An eye that beams a sweeter smile :
A bosom more enstrang'd from guile,
A heart with kinder passions warm'd,
A life with fewer stains deform'd ;
A death with deeper sighs confess'd
A memory more belov'd and bless'd.

ILIZEBETH
SMIH DyE^d oN
FEI^r ye 15 1727^8
AGE^d 25 yEAR
SAR^{nt} IOSE^h SMIH
DAVGH^{tr}

M^r
ELEAZAR WORNER
DyED ON MAY ye 8 1722 AGED 66 yEAR.

In Memory of
Mrs. SARAH MARSH,
wife of Ebenezer Marsh, who departed this life
January ye 31, 1794, in the 66th year of her age.

Prudence is an eveness of soul,
A steady temper, which no cares controul,
No passions ruffle, no desires inflame,
Still constant to itself, & still the same.

12

Rev. Jonathan Smith,
was settled in the ministry in
Chilmark, Martha's Vineyard, Jan. 23, 1788,
was dismissed by his desire on account of ill health,
Sept. 4th, 1827,
and died in Hadley, his native place,
April 14, 1829, Æ 31.

Reader, pause at this stone,
Know that thou art mortal,
And raise now one penitential
Cry for Mercy in thy dying hour.

Rev. John Brown,
Died March 22, 1839,
Æ 53 years,
8 years pastor of the 1st church in Hadley.

"They that be wise, shall shine as the brightness of the firmament; and they that turn many to righteousness as the stars forever and ever."

Note.—His wife Sarah M. and six children, are interred by his side; they all died between 1837, and 1842. At the bottom of the last monument is the following line,
"We are all here, and it is well."

In Memory of
Chester Smith,
son of Mr. Joseph and Mrs. Eunice Smith,
who was instantly killed by the
upsetting of a load of wood,
Jan. 25th, 1810, aged 18 years.

"Suddenly Death threw forth his dart,
"The fatal arrow pierced my heart,
"When health and vigor crown'd my day,
"Alas my soul was snatch'd away."

Mrs. Elizabeth,
Relict of Capt. Moses Porter,
who was born at East Hartford,
Oct 4th, AD 1719,
and died at Hadley, Oct. 2, 1798.

To the Memory of
John Webster, Esq,

One of the first settlers of Hartford, in Connecticut, who was many years a magistrate or assistant, & afterwards Deputy Governor of that Colony, & in 1659, with three sons, Robert, William & Thomas, associated with others in the purchase and settlement of Hadley, where he died in 1661. This monument is erected, in 1818, by his descendant, Noah Webster, of Amherst.

Here lies the body of the
Rev. Isaac Chauncy,

Pastor of the first church in Hadley, who was of a truly peaceable and Catholic spirit, a good scholar, an eloquent orator, an able divine, a lively, pathetic preacher, a burning and shining light in this candlestick, an exemplary christian, an Israelite indeed, in whom was no guile He departed this life 2 May, A. D. 1745, ætat. 74.

Here rests the body of the
Hon Eleazer Porter, Esq.

A lover of his country and universally benevolent. He compassionated the distressed, relieved the poor, was the orphan's friend, a kind husband, tender parent, a lover of good men, and an exemplary christian. He died, 6 Nov. 1757, anno ætatis 59.

Sacred to the memory of the
Rev. Samuel Hopkins, D. D.

Who, in christian duty exemplary, in friendship frank and sincere, in prudence and meekness eminent; able in counsel, a pattern of piety and purity, ever upright and honourable in conduct, the epitome of the heart; as a peacemaker blessed, as a minister of Christ, skilful and valiant in the truth; having, with ability and charity, long magnified his holy office, and served God and his generation faithfully; fell asleep, 8 March, A. D. 1811, in the 82 year of his age, and the 57 of his ministry.

In Memory of
Rev. Isaac Lyman,

The social, venerable, and pious pastor of the first church in York, for more than sixty years; was born at Northampton, Massachusetts, 25 February, 1724; graduated at Yale College, 1747; ordained 10 Dec. 1749; and died 12 March, 1810, ætat 85.

WEST SPRINGFIELD.

I saw an aged man upon his bier,
His hair was thin and white, and on his brow
A record of the cares of many a year ;--
Cares that were ended and forgotten now.
And there was sadness round, and faces bowed,
And woman's tears fell fast, and children wailed aloud.

Then rose another hoary man and said,
In faltering accents, to that weeping train,
Why mourn ye that our aged friend is dead?
* * * * * *
I am glad, that he has lived thus long,
And glad that he has gone to his reward ;
Nor deem, that kindly nature did him wrong,
Softly to disengage the vital cord.
When his weak hand grew palsied, and his eye
Dark with the mist of age, it was his time to die.—W. C. Bryant.

NOTE.—The Old Burying ground is about half a mile west of the Rail Road Bridge on Connecticut River.

[Inscription on the oldest Monument.]

HERE LyES THE BODy oF
MR. NATHANiEL DWiT,
who DIED at Springfield November the 7th 1711
in the 47th year of his age.

NOTE.—It probably was intended for Nathaniel Dwight, see note, page 130.

Here lyeth the Body of
DEACON JOHN BARBER
who Dyed INA^{RY} ye 17 1712
aged 70 years.

Here lyeth the Body of THO
MAS BARBER who
dyed Janu^y ye 16 1714 aged
40 years.

EPITAPHS. 137

In Memory of THRE daughters of
Mr Gideon & Mrs Mary Leonard
viz Cynthia died Sepr 26 1776
in the 4th year of her age
Tamer who died Sept 18 1776
aged 2 years.
Mary who died Aug 2^d 1777
in the 11th month of her age.

Here lyes interred the Body o
Ens^N John Ely
who deceased May 22^d 1754
in the 47th year of his age.

In Memory of
Dea^N John Ely
who died 15 Jany 1758
in the 80th year of his age.
"Reader behold as you pass by,
As you are now so once was I,
As I am now so you must be,
Prepare to die and follow me."

In Memory of
ye widow Mercy Ely
Consort of Dea^n John Ely
who died ye 5th of May 1763
in ye 83^d year of her age.

Here lyes interred
The Body of Mr. Caleb Ely
who deceased May ye 16 A D 1754
in ye 40th year of his age.

In Memory of
Samuel Ely
who died Decr ye 8th 1758
in the 58th year of his age.

12*

EPITAPHS.

Here lyeth the Body of
Mrs rebeccah EudNS
who dy^d the 1th day of Feb^r
uary ANOD 1739
in the 42^d year of her age.

Here lyeth the Body of
MRS MARy eLy
The wife of Deac^n IOSEPH eLy
who died the 19th of May
in the 71 year of her age
1 7 3 6.

In Memory of
W^D MARy ELy
Relict of Mr CALEB ELy
who died 7th Mar^h 1783
in the 62 year of her age.

In Memory of
Mrs Dorcas
wife of Mr John Ely
who died 3^d July 1777
in the 42 year of her age.
Also
of Mrs Eunice WHITE
RELECT OF ENS^N
IOHN ELy & ROG^R
WOLCOTT ESQ
who died at Bolton 29 March 1778
aged 73 years
Being the wife of JOEL WHITE ESQ.

Here is intered the Body of
Mr. Benjamin Stebbins,
who died Oct. ye 17th, 1748,
in the 72d year of his age.

In Memory of
Mr. BENJAMIN STEBBINS,
who died 11th Sept. 1783,
in the 82d year of his age.

"Death is debt to nature soul,
"Which I have paid and so must you."

In Memory of
Mr BENJAMIN ASHLEY
who died May 11 1772
in ye 76th year of his age.

"Were death deny'd the Saints would live in vain,
Death frees him from a world of Sin and Pain,
What Eden lost death gives with vast increase,
This King of terrours is the Prince of Peace.

---

1 7 1 4
MARY ELY.

In Memory of
ANNA, daugh^r of
Mr. Justin Ely, and Mrs. Ruth Ely,
died Jan. 6th, in 1776,
in the 9th year of her age.

Smitten friends, are Angels sent on errands full of love.

In Memory of three children, of
Mr. Martin and Mrs. Elizabeth Ely,
viz. an Infant born and decesed 7th June, 1774,
Also SETH, their son who died
3d Oct. 1776, aged 16 Months,
and PAMLIA, their daughter who died
26 April, 1787, aged 4 Months and 11 days.

EPITAPHS.

In Memory of
Mr. SAMUEL ELY, who died
Dec. 8th, 1758, in the 58th year of his age.
"Know then this truth
"Enough for man to know,
"Virtue alone is happiness below."

Here lies the body of
Mr. SAMUEL DAY,
who died Oct. ye 19, 1729,
in the 59th year of his age.

Here lies intered the Body of
Maior JOHN DAY,
who departed this life
October Novem. the 29, AD 1752,
in the 80th year of his age.

Here lies intered ye Body of
Mrs. MARY DAY,
wife of Major John Day,
who departed this life Feb. the 28th, 1742,
aged 65 years.

In Memory of
Lieut. NATHAN MORGAN,
who died August 12th, 1784,
in the 62d year of his age.
"O let my mouldering members teach
"What mortals ought to learn,
"For dust and ashes loudest preach,
"Man's Infinite concern."

NOTE.—The above Epitaph was written by the late venerable Doctor Lathrop.

In Memory of
Mr. DAVID BAGG,
who died May ye 19th 1760,
in ye 50th year of his age.

```
┌─────────────┐
│      M      │
│   MAyiOR    │
│    IOHN     │
│     ELy     │
└─────────────┘
```

In Memory of
Mr. Thomas Miller,
who died Sep. 8th 1781,
in the 94th year of his age.
Also
Mrs. Abigal, his wife died 1748,
in the 64th year of her age.

In Memory of
John Andrew Isense,
Born in little Biwene,
was a Dragoon in the Prince of Brunswicks Regt.
who was killed by lightning, Aug. 16th, 1780,
in the 28th year of his age.
"Ich weis Dasmein Ertoeser Leptund, er wird Mich wieder dus der erden Auferwecken." Job Capt 19th 25th.

Note.—Joseph and Tilley Mirrick, were under the tree when it was struck with Lightning; they were both knocked down.

Dea. Joseph Mirrick remained speechless several days. The *British Dragoon Isense* was some 20 feet from the tree, when he was killed, having taken shelter from the storm under a cock of hay.

In Memory of
Dea. Joseph Mirrick,
who with reputation and honour discharged the
varied duties of his christian and official character,
calmly fell asleep, 5th March, 1792,
in the 88th year of his age, and 42d of his Office.

Note.—On this stone the name is spelt Mirrick, on the others, Mirick. Within the last 50 or 60 years, it has been gradually changed to Merrick.

Here lies inter'd the Body of
Mrs. MARY, the Virtuous Consort of
Deacon Joseph Mirrick,
who deceased Jan. 3d 1779,
in her 73d year.

Reader behold as You pass by,
As you are now so once was I;
As I am now so You must be;
Prepare for Death and follow me.

Here lyeth the Body of
Mrs. SARAH MIRICK,
the wife of Lieut James Mirick,
who dyed Feb. y° 5th 1734,
in the 56th year of her age.

In Memory of
Lieut. JAMES MIRICK,
who died Sep. 8th, 1765,
in y° 95th year of his age.

In Memory of
Miss SUSAN, daughter of
Mr. Nehemiah and Mrs. Alice Rumrill,
who died Feb. 28th, 1786, aged 13 years.

"My fellow youths
"Remember you must die,
"And lay your heads as low as I."

[Copied from Monuments in the New Cemetery on the hill.]

In Memory of
Mrs. ELENOR, Consort of Mr. Joseph Ashley,
who died 14th April, 1808, in the 86th year of her age.

NOTE.—The first person interred in this Cemetery.

JOSEPH ASHLEY,
Died April 8, 1813, in the 93d year of his age.

LONGMEADOW.

"Life is real! Life is earnest!
And the grave is not its goal;
'Dust thou art, to dust returnest,'
Was not spoken of the soul.

Lives of great men all remind us,
We can make our lives sublime,
And, departing, leave behind us
Footprints on the sands of time:

Footprints, that perhaps another,
Sailing o'er life's solemn main,
A forlorn and shipwrecked brother,
Seeing, shall take heart again."--H. W. Longfellow.

[The oldest Monument in this Burying ground was removed from Springfield in May, 1848, by Mr. David Booth.]

MARy COLTON
ALiAS MARy DRAK(e)
WHO DyED Octo 10th 1682.
My DAyES AR^E
FEW. My GLAS IS RVN
My AGE 32 AND ONE
yET AM i INTH ARMS oF
My REDEEMER STRONG.

In Memory of
Mrs EXPERIENCE
ye wife of Mr Thomas
Hale who died
Sept 12th 1719
in her 42^d year.

" My days are past my purposes are broken off."

Betwen the above named
lies HEZEKIAH their Son
who died Jany 8th 1720
aged 4 months.
Our rest together is in the grave.

EPITAPHS.

Here Lyes
The Body oF
Mrs Elizabeth KEEP
who died the 29 day of July
1720 in the 12 year of her age.
EAR you young So Am i
Ther fore AL PRepare to die
The finest flesh is but dust—
Prepare,—for follow me you must.

Here lies intered the Body of
Capt. THOMAS COLTON,
who departed this life Sep. the 30, 1728,
aged 77 years, PROV 7.
The Memory of the just is blessed.

Here Lyeth the Body of
JOHN GUNN, of Westfield.
QUARTER MASTER,
who died Sep. 17, 1736,
aged about 82 years.

Here lies intered the Body of
Deac. NATHANIEL BURT,
who died on the 19th of July, 1749,
in ye 86th year of his age.
He was useful in life and had honour done him at his death,
Nathaniel the gift of God.—John, 1 : 47. Behold an Israelite indeed.

In Memory of
Mr. SOLOMON, son of
Lieut. David and Mrs. Mary Burt,
who was suddenly killed by the blowing
up of a powder mill, May 7th, 1777,
in his 19th year.
"Here is a voice directed here,
To old and young and all
That they be ready to appear,
Whenever Christ shall call."

In Memory of
Capt. Isaac Colton,
who died Jan. 23d 1757,
in his 57th, year.

Capt. J. Colton had a military genius, commanded a company at Louisburgh in 1745, was respected and useful at home, was a man of prayer.—Isaiah, 31 : 3. "For behold the Lord doth take away the Captain."

How art thou fallen in the midst of battle, O very pleasant hast thou been.

In Memory of
Lieut. Nathaniel Burt,
who was slain in the
memorable battle of Lake George,
Sep. 8th, 1755

When his Colonel and other brave officers fell, yet a signal victory was obtained over the enemy. Mr. Nathaniel Burt was a deacon of this church, an exemplary christian, a man of public spirit, and a good soldier, well beloved at home and in ye army. A concern for pure religion caused his going into ye military service. He died in his 45th year.—2 Chron. 35, and 25, and Jeremiah lamented over Josiah.

Sacred to the Memory of the
Rev. Richard S. Storrs,
pastor of the church in Longmeadow,
he was born at Mansfield, Conn. Aug. 30th, 1763,
graduated at Yale College in 1783,
ordained Dec. 7, 1785, died Oct. 3, 1819.

In the private relations of life he eminently illustrated the graces of the christian. He was distinguished for his appropriate, perspicuous, and affectionate exhibition of evangelical truth, for propriety, richness and fervor in social prayer, and for his instructive conversation and christian sympathy in pastoral duties. In testimony of their affectionate remembrance of his personal worth and their regard for his ability, zeal and usefulness as their christian pastor, his mourning congregation erect this monument.

AGAWAM.

He was there—
Swathed in that linen vesture for the grave—
The same loved one in all his comeliness—
And with him to the grave her heart must go.
What though he talk'd of her to angels? nay—
Hover'd in spirit near her?—'twas that arm,
Palsied in death, whose fond caress she knew!
It was that lip of marble with whose kiss,
Morning and eve, love hemm'd the sweet day in.—WILLIS.

The oldest Monument in Agawam.

In Memory of
Mrs. MARY,
Wife of Capt. Jon^a Worthington,
who died 10th May, 1794, aged 44 years.

Also of SETH,
their Son, who died 6th March, 1793,
in the 3d year of his age.

In Memory of
HARRIET,
who was MURDERED
By her Husband Samuel Leonard,
Dec. 14, 1825, Æ 33.

Also DELIA,
their dau^{tr}, Died Dec. 23, 1825,
Æ 13 ms.

"O sacred source of everlasting light,
Conduct the weary wanderer in her flight,
Direct her onward to that peaceful shore,
Where peril, pain, and death are felt no more."

In Memory of
Mr. Elnathan Baldwin,
who was suddenly killed by the wheel of a waggon,
near Hartford, on the 13 of July, 1812,
aged 40 yEARS.
Useful in Life,
AND LAMENTED In DEATH.
" The cup that my Father giveth me, shall I not drink it."
" Come all you weary travelers
Pray stop and drop a tear,
As I traveled I made a full stop here."

In Memory of
Capt. Jon^a Worthington,
who died 14th Augst 1809,
aged 65 years.

In Memory of
Mrs. Phœbe,
Wife of Mr. Jonathan Worthington,
who died May 17, 1809, aged 27.
Also an Infant babe.
" Depart dear friends, dry up your tears,
I must lie here till Christ appears."

In Memory of
Mrs. Sybil Worthington,
Consort of Cap^n Jona^a Worthington,
who with a new born son died 29th Mar^h, 1803,
aged 43 years.
ALSO
Another Infant Son,
who died 19th April, 1796,
aged 10 days.

While cold and lifeless lies the speechless form,
Which once was with each God-like virtue warm,
Which for the poor and needy wrought relief,
And lost its sufferings in another's grief;
Applauding seraphs hail thy happier shade,
To brighter realms, where no rude storm invades.

"Lucy,"
Daughter of Amos and Dezire Worthington,
Died June 15, 1846, Æ 41.

"She rests in peace, hushed is her voice,
Dim is her eye of light and love,
But let one thought your heart rejoice,
She's happy in the courts above."

JOB,
Son of Mr. Amos and Mrs. Dezire Worthington,
was drowned 14th April, 1804,
aged 16 Months.

In Memory of
Mr. JOHN WORTHINGTON,
who died April 15th, 1815,
in the 63 year of his age.

Also his daughter, ABi,
who died May 16, 1803,
aged 16 months.

EXTRACT FROM ANCIENT RECORDS.

"February the 14, 1638.

"Wee the Inhabitants of *Agaam* upon Quinnetticot takinge into consideration the manifold inconveniences, that may fall upon us, for want of some fit magistracy among us. Being now, by Gods Providence, fallen into the line of the Massachusetts jurisdiction; and it being farr off to repayre thither, in such cases of Justice, as may often fall out among us, doe therefore think it meett by a general consent and vote, to ordaine, (till we receive further directions from the General Court, in the Massachusetts Bay,) Mr. William Pynchon, to execute the office of a magistrate, in this our plantation of *Agaam*. viz. To give oaths to constables and military officers, to direct warrants, both processes, executions, and attachments, to hear and examine *misdemenor*, to inflict corporal punishment, as whipping, *stockinge*, byndinge to the peace or good behaviour, and in some cases, to require surcties, or if the offence require it to commit to prison, and in defaults of a comon prison, to commit delinquents to the charge of some fit person or persons till Justice may be satisfied."

WESTFIELD.

'Tis a harsh world, in which affection knows
No place to treasure up its loved and lost
But the foul grave! Thou, who so late wast sleeping
Warm in the close fold of a mother's heart,
Scarce from her breast a single pulse receiving
But it was sent thee with some tender thought,
How can I leave thee—*here!* *l*—WILLIS.

The oldest Mounment in Westfield.
HERE LyETH THE
BODy OF ABIGAIL
THE WIFE OF
JOHN NOBLE WHO
DIED IVLy 3 ANO
1683 in ye 20 YEAR
OF HER AGE.

IOHN
ROOT AGED
ABOVT 44 yEA^{RS}
HE DyED THE 24th
oF SEPT 1687.

Here lyeth buried the
Body of Mrs. MARGARET,
Wife of Mr. Samuel Taylor,
who was born May the 22d, 1836,
and dyed Sept. the 7th, A. D. 1708.

13*

Here lyeth intered the
Body of Mr. SAMUEL TAYLOR,
who was born August the 27th, ANNO DOM 1675,
and dyed April the 8th, A. D. 1709.

Here rests ye body of
Rev^d Mr. EDWARD TAYLOR,
Ye aged, venerable, Learned & Pious Pastor of ye Church of
Christ in this town, who, after He had served God and
his generation faithfully for many years, fell asleep
June 24th, 1729, in ye 87th year of his age.

Ensign
STEVEN KELLOGG,
Departed this life June ye VI, 1722,
in ye 55th year of HIS AGE.

In Memory of
Mrs RHODA, wife
of Deacon E L D A D
Taylor, died June ye 22d, 1740,
in ye 29th year of her age.
" A law eternal doth decree,
That all things made shall mortal be."

Here lyeth the
Body of MR. NOAH SHELDEN,
who died Augst 30, A. D. 1748,
aged 43 years.

In Memory of the
Hon. ELDAD TAYLOR, Esq ,
who died in Boston, 21st May, 1777,
Ætat 69, and lies in the tomb of the
Hon. John Wendell, Esq.
Also Mrs. THANKFUL TAYLOR, his Relict,
died 12th August, 1803, Ætat 82.

Kind Reader, this Stone informs you who we *ware*: what we
were, we tell you not, what we ought to have been, that be thou.
Where we now are you will know hereafter. Remember that
Christ is the Resurection and the Life.

EPITAPHS. 151

In Memory of
Mrs. RUTH,
Relict of ye Reverend Mr. Edward Taylor,
Died January ye 27th, 177*,
in the ** of her age.

"Hope humbly then, with trembling pinions soar,
Wait the GREAT Teacher Death, & God adore."

Here was buried the
Body of Mr. MOSES ROOT,
the Son of Mr. John & Mrs. Elizabeth Root,
who died Octo^{br} the 7th, A. D. 1744,
in the 28th year of his age.

EZRA,
SON oF MR. EZRA & MARGARET Clap,
Died Jan. ye 19th, 1754,
aged 20 ***.

Paul INGERSOL,
was born June the 19th, 1745,
and died the 5th day July next,
Son to Mr. Ezra & Mrs. ***.

This Stone stands to perpetuate
THE MEMORy oF
MAJ. MATHEW IVES,
who was born at Meriden, Ct., June 26, 1773,
and died FEB. 21, 1840.

To the Memory of
REV. JOSEPH MIX,
formerly Pastor of the Church in
West Suffield, Con.,
who died Aug. 4, 1833,
Ætat 68.

"In Christ is my hope, for Christ is the end of the law for righteousness to every one that believeth."

ELIZA BISHOP,
Born at Farmington, Ct., Dec. 9, 1813.

The five last years of her life were successfully devoted to the interests of Female Education & Piety, & amidst a wide & extended sphere of usefulness, died while Preceptress of Westfield Academy, April 26, 1839.

PORTER FOWLER,
Died October 12th, 1828,
aged 39 years.

In Memory of Mrs. THANKFUL,
the wife of Mr. Alexander Grant,
and Daughter of Mr. Gad Lyman, of Northampton,
who died Sept. 9, Anno Domini, 1770,
in the 25th year of her age.

Christ's dying Saints shall live again,
And in his kingdom ever reign.

Hon. WILLIAM SHEPERD,
Died Nov. 16th, 1817, aged 80.

He fought the battles of his country, aided the councils of our nation, and exemplified the character of the christian. The righteous shall be in everlasting remembrance.

In Memory of
CAPT. JOHN INGERSOLL,
who being in the service of his country,
was killed at Lake George, Sept. — 1755,
in the — year of his age.

In Memory of
Deaⁿ JOSEPH ROOT,
who died 7th June, 1779,
in the 74th year of his age.

Now after death my very dust will bid you come and share the love my soul did taste in the house of prayer.

EPITAPHS. 153

This Monument is erected to yᵉ Memory of
CAPT. JOHN MOSELY,
who departed this life on the first day of Sept. A. D. 1781,
in the 56th year of his age.

When virtue falls a victim to the grave,
In life distinguished by the wise and brave.
Let friendship deck its urn with choicest flowers,
Let melancholy mark the lonely hours;
In every breast let pity heave a sigh,
And feel the solemn truth that all must die,
Mingle with dust, and in earth's cold bosom lie.

In Memory of
GENERAL WAREHAM PARK,
who died March 6, 1801,
aged 49 years.

In Memory of
EDMUND ELY,
who died Jan'y 7, 1834,
Æ 71 years.

Also FRANKLIN,
Son of Edmund and Huldah Ely,
who was killed on board the U. S. Frigate Fulton,
at Brooklyn, N. Y., on the 4th day of June, 1829,
Æ 25 years.

Sacred to the Memory of Mrs.
MARGARET,
Consort of Dr. David Sheperd, of Chester,
who died Feb'y 10th, 1769,
in the 20th year of her age.

Many are the shapes of death, and many are the ways that lead
to his GRIM CAVE—all dreadful! But

Virtue alone assures that peace,
Which age nor death can destroy,
Afford the mind a lasting ease,
And fill it with immortal joy.

In Memory of
Mrs. ANNE,
Wife of Capt. John Kellogg,
and Daughter of Ephraim Terry, Esq.,
who died Oct. 3d, 1764, and in the 33 year of her age.

Also her infant Babe,
lying in her breast.

In Memory of the
Rev. JOHN BALLANTINE,
late Pastor of the Church of Christ in this place,
who died Feb'y 12th, 1776, in the 60th year of his age.

Mark the perfect and behold the upright, for the end of that man is peace.

Here lies interred the body of the
Rev. Mr. NEHEMIAH BULL,
who departed this life April 12th, 1740,
in the 39th year of his age.

In Memory of
COL. JAMES TAYLOR,
who died 14th Aug. 1803, aged 53 years.

Neither nobleness of mind, nor a feeling, generous heart, nor tears of friends, nor great usefulness in life, can secure any mortal from the arrest of death.

In Memory of
JOHN ASHLEY, ESQ.,
who died April ye 16th, 1759,
in ye 90th year of his age.

JAMES N.,
Eldest Son of Ira and Lucy Yeomans,
who was instantly killed when on his way to
school, by the slide of a bank of earth,
Nov. 20, 1840, Æ 7 1-2 years.

In Memory of
Mr. BENJAMIN,
Son of Deac. Benjamin and Mrs. Mary Dyer,
of Windham, Ct , who was drowned at Westfield,
July 11, 1805, aged 18 years.

In Memory of
Miss SUBMIT LYMAN,
who was killed by the fall of a tree, on the 9th Jan'y, 1797,
aged 29 years.
Death gives us more than we in Eden lost,
The King of Terrors, the Prince of Peace.

ZENAS ATKINS,
was suddenly killed while riding in a sleigh,
and coming in contact with another turning a corner,
on the evening of Jan'y 14th, 1816, aged 34.

HON. SAMUEL FOWLER, was born Sept. 5, 1747, and died Nov. 26, 1823.	JEMIMA FOWLER, his wife, was born Feb'y 5, 1761, and died Feb'y 28, 1826.

In Memory of
Mr. SAMUEL FOWLER,
who died Nov. 10, 1744, in his 61st year.
Hope humbly then, with trembling pinions soar,
Wait the great teacher Death, and God adore.

NOTE.—The Indian name of Westfield was Warronoco, and belonged to Springfield.

1658. Dec. The inhabitants of Springfield granted a tract of land to Thomas Cooper, on condition that he commenced improvements in 12 months, and continued them 5 years.

1660. A similar grant was made to Deac. S. Chapman.

1661. Another grant to Capt. Pyncheon, Robert Ashley, and George Colton.

1664. Feb'y 7. A committee was chosen by the citizens of Springfield, to take the charge of affairs at Warronoco, and to grant lands.

Some improvements were made as early as 1660, but no permanent settlers.

1666. Rev. Mr. Ballentine, in his private journal, April 8, 1754, says—"Died, Benjamin Saxton, aged 88, the first English child born in this town."

1667. Sept. 22. "Born, Mary, daughter of John and Mary Root," which is the first birth recorded. Meetings were first held this year on the Sabbath. Mr. Elizur Holyoke, of Springfield, preached six months.

1668. January. Rev. Moses Fish, of Chelmsford, came and preached 3 years.

1669. The town was incorporated. 9th month, 27th day, Moses Cook married to Elizabeth Clark. This is the first marriage on the records.

1671. 10th month, 3d day, Rev. Edward Taylor came here. The following heads of families were here at this date—John Pander, David Ashley, John Ingersoll, Moses Cook, Isaac Phelps, Edward Neill, Thomas Bancroft, Walter Lee, Thomas Dewy, John Osborn, Thomas Gunn, Gideon Green, Joseph Whiting, John Greet, and John Root.

1679. Last Wednesday of June the church was organized, and Mr. Taylor ordained. Seven men were selected to be formed into a church, called foundation men. Thomas Green was chosen, but declined; he was afterwards admitted to the church without narrating his experience, because he was "so decayed by age that it was hard to gather it."

1726. Oct. Mr. Nehemiah Bull was ordained colleague pastor with Mr. Taylor.

1741. June 17. Rev. John Ballentine, of Boston, was ordained pastor.

1781. Nov. 22. Rev. Noah Atwater was ordained. He kept 20 sermons on hand, never preached the same to his own people a second time, and had his sermon for the ensuing Sabbath ready on Tuesday evening.

1800. Jan'y 1st. Westfield Academy was dedicated, and the institution opened under the superintendence of Peter Starr, now in Middlebury, Vt Sermon by Dr. Lathrop.

1803. Nov. 16. Rev. Isaac Knapp, of Norfolk, Ct., was ordained.

1806. Jan'y 1st The present Congregational Church was dedicated. Sermon by Mr. Knapp. Text Gen. 28, 17. May, a Baptist church organized. The one organized in 1784 had become extinct.

1836. June 1. Rev. Emerson Davis was ordained colleague with Mr. Knapp.

1844. Sept. Normal School opened at Westfield.

1846. Sept. 3d. The Normal School building dedicated.

1847. July 6. Died, Rev. Isaac Knapp, aged 72.

HAYDENVILLE.

The only Monument in this Village.
Family Monument.
JOSIAH HAYDEN,
Died July 26, 1847,
aged 79 years.
" Strong in faith, giving glory to God;"

WILLIAMSBURGH.

"OUR FATHERS, WHERE ARE THEY?"
" Beneath those rugged elms, that yew tree's shade,
Where heaves the turf in many a mouldering heap,
Each in his narrow cell forever laid,
The rude forefathers of the hamlet sleep."—GRAY'S ELEGY.

The oldest Monument in Williamsburgh.
Mr. THOMAS NASH,
Died March 12th,
1773, in ye 81 year of his age.

This Monument is sacred
to the Memory of the
Rev. AMOS BUTLER,
Who was born at Hartford; settled the first gospel minister in this town; sustained the ministerial character with uncommon dignity and usefulness four years; and rested from his labors Oct. 13th, 1777, in the 30th year of his age.
" If they hear not Moses and the prophets neither will they hear though one rose from the dead."

In Memory of
Mr. JOSIAH HAYDEN,
who died Dec. 29, 1810,
in the 78th year of his age.

Tho' mouldering in the dust I lie
I speak to all, prepare to die.

In Memory of
EDWARD GERE,
who died Sep. 24, 1832, Æ 34.

" Short toil, sore pain dear friend was thine,
Now joys eternal and divine."

Rev. DAVID E. GOODWIN,
Died May 2d, 1842, Æ 31.

Rev. CHESTER LORD,
Died Nov. 8, 1834, Æ 22.
Having just entered with promise upon the ministry.

To the Memory of
Rev. JOSEPH STRONG,
who died Jan. 1, 1803,
in the 74th year of his age,
and 52d of his ministry.

Naturally possessed of great self command, a correct judgment and a penetrating mind; he was eminently qualified for ruling a church and silencing opposers; by a faithful examination of the scriptures he acquired a thorough knowledge of their truths; and in his discourses taught them with perspicuity and force. His ministry, by a divine blessing, was crowned with remarkable success.

In Memory of
Mrs. JANE STRONG,
wife of Rev. Joseph Strong,
who died Sept. 21st 1811,
in the 83d year of her age.

EPITAPHS.

Rev. HENRY LORD,
for 30 years pastor of
The First church in Williamsburgh,
Died Nov. 22, A. D. 1834, Æ 53.

He was a faithful minister of Christ and an example of modesty, gentleness, punctuality, simplicity and godly sincerity.

Mrs. FIDELIA,
wife of Rev. H. Lord,
Died 25 Nov. 1828, Æ 35.

WESTHAMPTON.

"Moments seize,
Heaven's on their wing; a moment we may wish,
When worlds want wealth to buy."—YOUNG.

The oldest Monument.
In Memory of
Mrs. SARAH THAYER,
Wife of Mr. Zebulon Thayer,
who died Jan. 23d, 1786,
in the 84th year of her age.
Pray stop my friends * *
* * * *

Mr. JOHN PARSONS,
the first person buried in this yard,
Died March 23d, 1791,
Ætat 46.

"Passenger, see what numbers die,
The old, the young, together lie,
And bless'd is he who ascends on high."

SYLVESTER JUDD, ESQ.,
Died Sept. 19, 1832, aged 79 years.

Mrs. Hannah Judd,
Consort of Sylvester Judd, Esq.,
and Daughter of Samuel Burt, of Southampton,
was born April 2, 1754, and died Jan. 27, 1821,
aged 66 yEARS.

She was an affectionate WIFE, a tender MOTHER, a kind FRIEND,
an exemplary CHRISTIAN.

In Memory of
Mrs. Lydia Parsons,
Consort of Mr. John Parsons,
who died Dec. 25, 1794,
aged 53.

She & her husband, Mr. John Parsons, were the first married couple buried in this yard.

In Memory of
Mrs. Eunice Clark,
Wife of Mr. Eben^r Clark,
who died Dec. 4th, 1791,
aged 40 years and 28 days.

Also their Children, who died as follows:
Rozel,
Died April 21st, 1779, aged 21 days.

Medad,
Died April 21st, 1791, aged 6 months and 17 days.

In Memory of
Mr. Thomas Clapp,
who died Sept. 27, 1797,
aged 35 years.

Sacred to the Memory of
Capt. Jared Hunt,
who died Sept. 24th, 1812,
in the 52d year of his age.

In Memory of
PAUL BULLARD,
Son of Mr. John & Mrs.
Joanna Bullard,
who was drowned
Aug. 23, 1796,
in the 18th year
of his age.

In Memory of
TIMOTHY EDWARDS,
Son of Mr. Timothy & Mrs
Thankful Edwards,
who was drowned
Aug. 23, 1796,
in the 12th year
of his age.

In Memory of
REV. ENOCH HALE,
who was Fifty-Six years the faithful and beloved
Minister of the Church in this town, and
OCTAVIA, his Wife.
Rev. Enoch Hale,
Born Oct. 28, 1753, at Coventry, Conn.,
Ordained Sept. 27, 1779, as the first
Pastor of the Church in this town.
Died Jan. 14, 1837, aged 84 years.
Erected in testimony of the
respect and gratitude of surviving Parishioners.
" He taught us how to live, and Oh! too high a price for
knowledge, taught us how to die."

OCTAVIA,
Wife of Enoch Hale, and Daughter of
Rev. Benj. Throop, Born July 7, 1754,
at Bozrah, Conn.,
Married Sept. 30, 1781,
Died Aug. 18, 1839, aged 85 years.

In Memory of
Mr. ASA THAYER,
who died March 14th, 1809,
in the 61st year of his age.

Remember all there's none can save,
The mortal body from the grave,
Yet weeping friends dry up your tears,
We shall awake when Christ appears.

EPITAPHS.

Mr. Timothy Edwards,
Died April 11th, 1834, aged 83 years.

Capt. Noah Cook,
Died May 23d, 1832, aged 75 years.

Mr. Solomon Judd,
Died Nov. 8th, 1830, in the 73d year of his age.

Hophni Judd, Esq.,
Son of Sylvester Judd, Esq., and Mrs. Hannah Judd,
was born July 8th, 1793, graduated at Williams College,
1812, admitted as Attorney at Law, 1816,
Died March 15th, 1818,
aged 24 years.

Beloved and respected in life, lamented in death.

In Memory of
Capt. Azariah Lyman,
who departed this life Oct. 23d, 1833,
aged 85 years.

Lord he was thine, and not our own,
Thou hast not done us wrong,
We thank thee for that precious loan,
Afforded us so long.

In Memory of
Mr. Peter Montague,
who died Sept. 24th, 1822, aged 71 years.

Note.—The Church in Westhampton was organized Sept. 1st, 1779—Rev. Enoch Hale was ordained as Pastor, Sept. 29th, 1779 : died Jan. 14, 1847.

Rev. Horace B. Chapin was installed as Colleague Pastor, July 8th, 1829 : dismissed May 1st, 1837.

Rev. Amos Drury was installed as Pastor, June 29th, 1837—died at Pittsford, Vt., July 22d, 1841.

Rev. David Coggin was ordained as Pastor, May 11th, 1842.

EASTHAMPTON.

"Our dying friends come o'er us like a cloud,
To damp our brainless ardors; and abate
That glare of life, which often blinds the wise.
Our dying friends are pioneers, to smooth
Our rugged path to death; to break those bars
Of terror, and abhorrence, nature throws
Cross our obstructed way: and, thus to make
Welcome, as safe, our port from every storm."—YOUNG.

[The oldest Monument in Easthampton.]

CATHERINE,
Daut^r of Mr. Stephen and Mrs. Catherine Wright,
Died FEB'RY 14th, 1761, in her 6th year.

"Behold He taketh away, who can hinder him? Who will say unto him what doest thou?"

In Memory of
MAJ^R Jonathan CLAP,
who died May 10th, 1782, in the 69 year of his age.

The wise, the just, the pious and the brave,
Live in their death, and flourish in the grave.
Here sown in death the body lies.
Till God shall call & bid it rise.

Mrs. SARAH,
ye wife of Mr. Ebenezer Corse,
Died Jan^r 3, 1768, in the 73 year of her age.

By Adam's sin we all must die,
By Christ alone we rise on high.

In Memory of
Capt. STEPHEN WRIGHT,
who died FEB^{RY} 15th, 1763, in ye 71 year of his age.

Blessed are the dead who die in the Lord; yea saith the spirit, that they may rest from their labours, and their works do follow them.

In Memory of
Mrs. ESTHER,
ye relict of Capt. Stephen Wright,
who died Nov. 26, A. D. 1770,
in ye 76 year of her age.

Mr. EBEN^R CORSE,
Died May 4th, A. D. 1776,
in ye 85 year of his age.

In Memory of
Mrs. ELISABETH,
ye wife of Mr. Josiah Parsons,
who died August 6th, 1775,
in the 78 year of her age.

In Memory of
CAPT. LUTHER CLAP,
who died August 17th, aged 39 years.
And his wife, Mrs. TIRZAH CLAP,
who died 31st same month, aged 38 years,
A. D. 1811.
Both fell victims to the Typhus FEVER.
They were active, pleasing, benevolent, devout.

For us no longer mourn,
Your souls demand your care,
Soon you will be hither borne,
For death, oh friends prepare.

Insatiate Archer, could not one suffice? Thy shaft flew twice, and twice it smote full sore. Scarce did the widow'd mourner from the cold grave of a lov'd partner trace her backward steps, than death his awful mandate sent to call her hence. Two weeks she struggled with disease, when death released her from suffering here, to soar on angel's wings to realms of bliss. This once happy pair who here repose, no children left their early exit to lament, but many friends who their sad fate will long bemoan. Rich in the comforts of domestic BLISS, blest with the ample gifts of FORTUNE, and more bless'd with ample hearts disposed to sweetest acts of CHARITY.

SOUTHAMPTON.

"Death's admonitions, like shafts upward shot,
More dreadful by delay, the longer ere
They strike our hearts, the deeper is their wound"--YOUNG.

[The oldest Monument.]
Mr. Simeôn WAIT
Died * * * * y° 14th, 1738, yRS * * *

In Memory of
Mr. JOHN KINGSLEY,
who died April 30, 1756,
in y° 23 year of his AGE.

In Memory of
Mr. PHINEH^S KING,
who died Jan^{ry} 10th, 1768,
in the 62d year of his AGE.

In Memory of
Mr. ROGER CLAP,
who died Jan^r 3d, 1773,
in y° 65th year of HIS AGE.

In Memory of
Mrs. ANNY,
Wife of Mr. Roger Clap,
who died July 7, 1766,
in y° 54 year of HER AGE.

Sacred to the Memery of
LEMUEL POMEROY, ESQ..
who died Dec. 14th, 1819,
in the 82 year of HIS AGE.

Virtue outshines the stars, outlives the tomb,
Climbs up to heaven, and finds a peaceful home.

In Memory of
Mr. BENJAMIN LYMAN,
who died May 1st, 1762,
in the 60th year of HIS AGE.

In Memory of
Mrs. MARY,
Relict of Mr. Benjn Lyman,
who died August 17th, 1782,
in the 75th year of HER AGE.

REV. VINSON GOULD,
Died April 4th, 1841, Æ LXVII.

To the Memory of
REV. JONATHAN JUDD,
The first Minister of Christ in Southampton,
and of Mrs. SILENCE JUDD,
his amiable and worthy consort,
who died Oct. 25, 1783,
in the 63d year of her age.

He saw his people of 30 familys increase to nearly 1000 souls; was able, evangelical, and faithful in preaching; was eminent in piety, wisdom, meekness, benevolence; lived greatly respected and beloved, and after a Ministry of more than 60 years, rested from his labours July 28, 1803, in the 84th year of his age. May those who knew him imitate his faith and virtue, and when they depart have his hope of life. The lost will be found.

ALSO
Of four of their grand-children,
named SYLVESTER,
Sons of Sylvester Judd, Esq., & Mrs. Hannah Judd,
who died, the first June 1, 1775,
aged 12 hours.
The second Sept. 28, 1776,
aged 5 weeks.
The third Feb. 23, 1779, aged 24 hours.
The fourth April 15, 1780, aged 11 weeks.

EPITAPHS. 167

JONATHAN JUDD, ESQUIRE,
Died Jan. 30, 1819, in the 75 year of his age.
He was born Oct. 7, 1744, old style, & was graduated at Yale College, in 1765.
He was an honest man, a good citizen, an upright merchant, a judicious Magistrate, and faithful and benevolent in the duties of life. His virtues are still fondly recollected by his friends, and his brothers and sisters have the melancholly pleasure of bestowing this last tribute of affection to his worth, out of a small part of the property left them by him.
Jonathan Judd, Esqr. was the oldest son of the Rev. Jonathan Judd, the first Minister of the Gospel in Southampton, who was the son of William Judd, and Grandson of Thomas Judd, both of whom lived in Waterbury, Conn.

AMHERST.

"Room, gentle flowers! my child would pass to heaven!
Ye look'd not for her yet with your soft eyes,
O watchful ushers at Death's narrow door!
But lo! while you delay to let her forth,
Angels, beyond, stay for her."—WILLIS.

[The oldest Tomb Stone in Amherst.]

M^R.   E
IOIIN
SCOTT   G
DYE^D oN OC^T y^e
27th, 1737, AGE^D A
*   *   y—EAR oF
KINGS
MR.   TOWN
WILLIAM SCOT   SON   of
* * * *

In Memory of
the Rev^d Mr. DAVID PARSONS,
First Pastor of the Church at Amherst,
who died January 1, 1781, in the 69 year of his age,
and 41st of his Ministry.

A man of God and faithful servant of Jesus Christ. Rev. 14, 13.
Blessed are the dead that die in the Lord ; yea, saith the
Spirit, their works do follow them.

In Memory of
Mrs. EUNICE PARSONS,
Consort of the Rev. David Parsons,
who died Sept. 20th, 1796, in ye 94 y^r of her age.

Let me interpret for him, me his advocate and propitiation, all his
works in me, good or not good, ingraft ; my merit those
shall perfect ; and for these my death shall pay.

REV. ROYAL WASHBURN,
Born at Royalton, Vt., Dec. 6, 1797,
graduated at Vermont University, 1820,
and at the Andover Theologigal Seminary, 1824,
settled as Pastor of the first church and parish, Amherst,
Jan. 4, 1826, died Jan. 1, 1833.

Honored and beloved in the church, having a good report of them
without ; seeming blameless as the steward of God ; in doctrine
showing sincerity and sound speech, in practice a pattern of
good works ; yet lowly of heart, and ascribing all to the
grace of God through Christ ; his ministry short, but
blessed with joyous fruit ; his life as becometh saints ;
his death full of peace. Multum diuque desiderabimus.

In Memory of
REV. ICHABOD DRAPER.
He graduated at Harvard College, 1783,
was ordained over the 2d East Parish, in this town, 1785,
dismissed in 1809,
and died Dec. 17, 1827,
aged 72.

The tall, the wise and reverend head must lie as low as ours.

Rev. Nathan Perkins,
Born at West Hartford, Con., Aug. 1777,
Graduated at Yale College, Sept. 1795,
Ordained over the 2d Congregational Church,
in Amherst, Mass., Oct. 10, 1810,
and died March 28th, 1842,
in the 66th year of his age, and the 33d of his ministry.
A sound and evangelical Preacher, an active Pastor, a Peacemaker—known and beloved in the Churches, and having a good report of them who are without.
" And I heard a great voice from heaven, saying unto me write, blessed are the dead who die in the Lord, from henceforth ; for they rest from their labors, and their works do follow them."

Rev. Pomeroy Belden,
Born March 15, 1811,
Grad. Amherst Coll. 1833,
Ordained Aug. 8, 1837,
was Minister of the Orthodox Society in
S. Deerfield, 5 years,
Installed Pastor of the Church in Amherst,
E. Parish, Sept. 14, 1842,
Died March 2, 1849.
For me to live is Christ, and to die is gain.

In Memory of
Mr. Solomon Boltwood,
who died April 20th, 1762, in ye 70th year of his age.

This Monument
is erected to ye memory of
Lieut. Solomon Boltwood, ye 3d,
who deceased Dec. 12th, A. D. 1805,
in ye 46th year of his age.
His death was occasioned by being suddenly thrown from a bridge, while raising ye same.
Be ye also ready, for in such an hour as ye think not the Son of man cometh.

15

In memory of
Doct. Seth Coleman,
who died Sept. 9, 1816, aged 76.

[Masonic Emblems.]
In memory of
Capt. Calvin Merrill,
who died 15th March, 1820, aged 55.
Why lingers hope around the silent dead,
There is another and a better world.

Gen. Ebenezer Mattoon,
Died Sept. 11, 1843, Æ 88.

Sarah,
daughter of Park & Joanna A. Warner,
Died March 3, 1828, Æ 1 day.

The Rev. Austin Dickinson,
was born in Amherst, Ms., Feb. 15, 1791,
Graduated at Dartmouth College, in 1813,
and after a life of eminent christian enterprise
and usefulness,
Died in the city of New York,
Aug. 15, 1849, aged 58.
A few friends have erected this Monument at his grave as a
tribute to his worth.

Samuel F. Dickinson,
Died at Hudson, O.
April 22, 1838, aged 62.
His wife
Lucretia G. Dickinson,
Died at Enfield, Mass.
May 11, 1840, aged 64.
Their remains were removed to this spot by their children.
'If a man die shall he live ? for if we believe that *Jesus* died and
rose again, even so them also which sleep in Jesus will God
bring with him.'

EPITAPHS. 171

Doct. Robert Cutler,
Died March 10, 1835, aged 86.

Dr. Isaac G. Cutler,
Died Nov. 29, 1834, aged 52.

Dr. William F. Sellon,
Died Dec. 31, 1842, Æ 56.

Simeon Strong, Esq.
(Judge of the Supreme Judicial Court
of the Commonwealth of Mass.)
Died December 14, 1805,
in the 70 year of his age.

Man but dives in Death; dives from the Sun in fairer days to
rise, the graves. * * *

Jonathan Kellogg,
Died Feb. 28, 1823, aged 63 years.

Mary,
wife of Jonathan Kellogg,
Died March 5, 1823, aged 61 years.

What though our bodies now entombed,
Are mouldering into dust,
A dying Jesus has perfumed
The graves of all the just.

Mrs. Lois,
wife of Mr. Chester Kellogg,
Died Dec. 13, 1809, aged 20 years.

Dwelt faith, love, and friendship here,
O, view the change and drop a tear.

Chester Kellogg,
Died January 7, 1849, Aged 61 years.

Ira Kellogg,
Died Nov. 16, 1843, aged 57 years.

Hic jacet corpus sepultum
Reverendi ZEPHANIÆ SWIFT MOORE, S. T. D.,
Collegit Amherstiæ Præsidus.

Ille homo ingenioque scientia, atque pietate sincera, præclarus; ac mentis gravitate quoque insigni quum se demittens. Animo et consilio certus, sed tamen mitissimus semperque facilitate permagna, modestus, placabilis, misericordia et fructibus bonis plenus. Non dijudicans, non simulator; discipulis suis veneratus quasi illis pater dilectusque. Maximo omnium desiderio mortem obiit, die XXX Jun., Anno Domini MDCCCXXIII. Ætatis suæ LIII. Hanoveriæ gradum Artium Bacalaurei admissus, anno Domini MDCCXCIII. Ecclasiæ Logecestriensis Pastor annos XIV, Collegii Dartmuthensis linguarum Professor IV, Colegii Gulielmi Præses II. Curatores Collegii Amherstiæ hoc saxum ponendum curavere.

[Translation.]

Here lies buried the body of the
Reverend ZEPHANIAH SWIFT MOORE, D.D,
President of the College at Amherst.

He was a man pre-eminent for genius, and science, and sincere piety, as well as greatness of mind and humility. He was firm in his purposes, and yet very mild, easy to be entreated, modest, placable, full of mercy and good works. He was not censorious, and no dissembler. By his pupils he was loved and venerated as a father. To the great grief of all, he died on the 30th of June, in the year of our Lord 1823, and in the 53d year of his age. He received the degree of Bachelor of Arts at Hanover in 1793; he was pastor of the church at Leicester 14 years, Professor of languages at Dartmouth College 4 years, President of Williams College 2 years. The trustees of the College at Amherst have ordered this stone to be erected.

Mr. TITUS WARNER,
Died 12 April, 1818, in his 59 year.

  "Vain man thy fond pursuits forbear,
  "Repent, thy end is nigh,
  "Death at the fartherest can't be far,
  "O, think before thou die.

EPITAPHS. 173

Mrs. Mary,
wife of Mr. Titus Warner,
Died Nov. 15, 1843, Æ 70

HATFIELD.

"Keep silence! be solemn! my life wears away —
E'en now I look down where my form they will lay,
Where oft I have wandered at close of the day
And silently mused o'er the dead;

Come, hie thee forth, sexton, with mattock and spade,
They've pointed the spot where my bones must be laid,
They've ordered my coffin and shroud to be made —
I go to my last narrow bed."—J. E. D. Comstock.

Sacred to the memory of that venerable man,
Deacon Obadiah Dickinson,
who early witnessed a good confession, who through
various dispensations, in prosperity and adversity,
exemplified the religion of Jesus;
who, for many years, used the office of a deacon well, and
purchased to himself a good degree and great
boldness in the faith, who, in the hope of a
better life, fell asleep, June, A. D. 1788,
in the 84th year of his age.
Is. 26, 19.

In memory of
the Hon. Israel Williams, Esquire,
who departed this life, 10 January, 1788,
in the 79 year of his age.
High and low, rich and poor, are death's equal prey, and no
valuable distinction survives his resistless attack, but
that, which ennobles an angel, the love of God.
All on earth is shadow, all beyond
Is substance; the reverse is folly's creed.
How solid all, where change shall be no more!

Interred the remains of
Mrs. SARAH WILLIAMS,
the daughter of the Hon. John Chester Esq.
and worthy consort of the Hon. Israel Williams, Esq.
she departed this life, the 18 of September, A. D. 1770,
aged 63 years.

In memory of
the REV. TIMOTHY WOODBRIDGE,
for 30 years Pastor of the Church of Christ,
in the town of Hatfield.

NOTE.—This man of God, who called on the Lord, out of a pure heart, followed after righteousness, godliness, faith, love, patience, meekness, apt to teach, charitable, and gentle to all men, departed this life, on the 3 of June, A. D. 1770, in the 58 year of his age.

To the memory of
Mr. JACOB WALKER,

who, respected by the brave, beloved by his country's friends, dear to his relations, while manfully defending the laws and and liberties of the Commonwealth, nobly fell by the impious hand of treason and rebellion, on the 17th of February, 1787, in the 32 year of his age.

NOTE.—This valiant friend of his country was killed in a dastardly manner, by one of the deluded followers of Shays in time of an alarming insurrection in New England.

In memory of
the HON. JOHN HASTINGS, ESQ.,

who, an early professor of the faith of Christ, observed strictly gospel ordinances; in perilous times faithfully performed the duties of the citizen patriot; for 36 years an upright magistrate, and for 28 years a Senator or Counsellor of this Commonwealth; was gathered to his fathers, 6 December, A. D. 1811, in the 74 year of his age. Her strong rods were broken and withered.—EZEKIEL.

Here lies interred the remains of
OLIVER PARTRIDGE, ESQ.,
who died the 21 of July, A. D. 1792,
in the 81 year of his age.
His usefulness in church and state,
Was early known to men;
Blest with an active life, till late,
And happy in his end.

NOTE.—The family of Partridge here interred are descendants from William Partridge, who came from Berwick on Tweed, in Great Britain, and died in Hadley. Oliver was the son of Edward, Edward was the son of Samuel, Samuel was the son of William, who was one of the first adventurers in forming settlements on Connecticut river in the 17th century.

Here are interred the remains of
Mrs. ANNA PARTRIDGE,
Consort of Oliver Partridge, Esq.,
who died 21 Dec. A. D. 1802, in the 86 year of her age.
In youth devoted to the Lord,
Through a long life, esteem'd his word;
Trusted in God, his laws obeyed,
And thus an happy exit made.

SOUTH HADLEY.

"The dead are there
And millions in these solitudes, since first
The flight of years began, have laid them down
In their last sleep — the dead reign there alone."—BRYANT.

JOHN PRESTON,
D y E^D ON MARCH
ye 4, 1727^8, AGED
41 yEAR, AND THE
FIRST HERE BURIED.

176　　　　　　EPITAPHS.

[On the only Tomb in the Grave Yard.]
HERE LIES ENTOMBED,
Col. Ruggles Woodbridge,
who died Mar. 8, 1819, Æt 80.

In Memory of the
Rev^d. John Woodbridge,
late Minister of the Gospel of Christ in this town,
who was born at Springfield, Dec. 25, 1702,
and died Sept. 10, 1783, in the 81st year of his age.
He was son of ye venerable and Reverend John Woodbridge, of Springfield, 2d Parish.

Mrs. Tryphena,
his first wife, died Jan'y 10, 1749,
in her 42d year.

Mrs. Martha,
his second wife, died Aug. 20, 1783,
in her 58th year.

This stone stands but to tell
Where their dust lies, and who they was.
When saints will rise, that day will show
The part they acted here below.

Sacred to the memory of
Rev. Joel Hayes,
who died July 29, 1827,
aged 74,
having been 45 years Pastor of the
Church in this place.

Blessed are the dead, &c.

In memory of
Lieut. Luke Montague,
A worthy Christian, and an ornament to the
community in general,
who died Aug. 23, 1775, in the 76th year of his age.

EPITAPHS. 177

NOTE.—THIS town was originally a parish in Hadley; it was incorporated as a town in 1753. Was settled as early as 1721 by a few families from Hadley. It was then called the South Precinct in Hadley. The first settlers for some time continued to attend public worship on the Sabbath in Hadley, a distance of about 7 or 8 miles. In 1733 the first town meeting as a separate district was held, and it was resolved that a meeting-house, the frame of which was put up the year before, should be in part finished. The building, however, was not completed until the close of the year 1737. The families were few in number and indigent in their circumstances, and the house was principally built by their labor; it was not large, containing only nine pews in the body of it. A gallery was subsequently added. There was no steeple or bell. The people were called together at the appointed hour of public worship by the " blowing of a conch shell." The house still remains, and is occupied as a dwelling house, on the north side of the common. In consequence of the house being too small to accommodate the people, at the meeting of the town in March, 1750, a vote was passed to build a new house, 55 feet in leng a and 45 in breadth, to be placed as near the old one as might conveniently be done, and as near the center of the town as possible. The difficulty of locating the house was without a parallel. It was not till *thirteen* years afterwards that the question was settled, during which more than fifty meetings for the purpose of agreeing on the place were held. It was finally settled by lot. The lot fixed the place where the meeting-house of the first parish now stands. A part being dissatisfied, a council of ministers was called, consisting of the Rev. Dr. Williams of Longmeadow, Rev. Mr. Breck of Springfield, Rev. Mr. Ballantine of Westfield, and Rev. Mr. Lathrop of West Springfield, who decided that both parties were under moral obligation to abide by the lot. The first pastor of the church in South Hadley was Rev. Grindall Rawson, who was settled in 1733. A grant of land, called the " *Proprietors' Land*," was set off to this town on its first settlement, by the town of Hadley, for the use of the ministry, on condition that the people would settle among them " a good orthodox minister." By a vote of the precinct, at their first meeting, this land was appropriated to Mr. Rawson. Rev. John Woodbridge, the successor of Mr. Rawson, was installed pastor in 1742. He died in 1783, aged 80. He was succeeded in the ministry by Rev. Joel Hayes, who was settled in 1782. Rev. Artemas Boies, the next minister, was settled in 1824. Rev. Joseph D. Condit was settled July 8, 1835, ob. Sept. 19, 1847. Rev. Thomas Laurie was settled June 7, 1848. Rev. Flavel Griswold was the first pastor of the second or *Canal church*. He was installed pastor in 1828; Rev. William Tyler succeeded him in 1832.

CHESTERFIELD.

"Leaves have their time to fall,
And flowers to wither at the north wind's breath,
And stars to set — but all,
Thou hast all seasons for thine own, O death!"—Mrs. HEMANS.

This town was incorporated 1762 — the Congregational Church was formed in 1764, Rev. BENJAMIN MILLS ordained Pastor same year, resigned 1774, Died 1785. Rev. JOSEPH KILBOURN, settled 1780, died within one year. Rev. TIMOTHY ALLEN, settled 1785, was Pastor of the Chnrch 10 years. Rev. JOSIAH WATERS, settled 1796 and continued as Pastor until 1831. Rev. ISRAEL G. ROSE, ordained 1836, died 1842. Rev. OLIVER WARNER Jun. ordained June 5, 1842, dissmissed Oct. 1846.

The first person buried in this town was the first wife of Col. BENJ. BONNY. It was then a wilderness; Mr. ABIL STETSON, cut out the brush in the woods and dug the grave.

In Memory
BENJAMIN MILLS Esq.,
first Minister of the Gospel in this town,
he died March 14, A. D. 1785,
in the 46 year of his age.

The sweet remembrance of the just,
Shall flourish when they sleep in dust,
Until here, they join above,
And never cease to praise and love.

In Memory of
Mrs. MARY MILLS,
the amiable consort of Benjamin Mills Esq.
she died June 30, A. D. 1779, aged 40 years.

If worth and virtue could retrieve from death,
She never had resigned her mortal breath.

In memory of
Mrs. PERSIS WHITE,
wife of Mr. Josiah White.
Also in memory of
Mrs. FRANCIS MERICK,
wife of Joseph Merick.
Mrs. White died Oct. 6, 1797, aged 31.
Mrs. Merick, Oct. 5, 1797, aged 27.

They were sisters, virtuous and lovely, as wives they were amiable, and as parents, they were kind and affectionate. In the midst of usefulness they were arrested by the harbinger of death. Nature sickened around them both at once, their eyes lost their lustre, the world its variegated charms, and they expired, one just 32 hours after the other.

Shew us thy face and we'll away
From all inferior things,
Speak Lord, and here we'll quit our clay,
And stretch our airy wings.

Mrs. HANNAH,
wife of Capt. Joseph Burnell,
died June 29, 1797
in the 72 year of her age.

Behold and see as you pass by,
As you are now, so once was I,
As I am now, so you must be,
Prepare for Death, and follow me.

To the memory of
DEACON BENJAMIN PRICE,
who died May 11, 1809,
in the 64 year of his age.

In memory of
BENJAMIN BRYANT,
who died Aug. 3, 1788, aged 54 years.

In memory of
MISS MARY WHITE,
Daughter of Esq. Asa and Zilpah White,
who died 28 Feb'y, 1814, aged 23.

In memory of
RUTH STETSON,
who died April 12th, 1809, in the 63d year of her age.

Also ABIEL STETSON,
who died Aug. 28th, 1819, in the 81st year of his age.

> Death leaves a melancholy gloom,
> It makes an empty seat,
> Ye living mortals all must come
> And try this long retreat.

In memory of
CAPT. JOSHUA HEALY,
who died May 23, A. D. 1791, aged 64 years.

> Here rests our friend, no more shall death
> Disturb his mind, or stop his breath,
> When the Judge comes, then he shall rise
> To meet his God, with sweet surprise.

In memory of
Mr. BENJAMIN,
Son of Mr. Seth and Mrs. Martha Taylor,
who died 28 July, 1797, in the 19 year of his age.

In memory of
Mr. STEPHEN BAKER,
who died April 29, 1813, in the 82 year of his age.

My flesh and my heart faileth, but God is the strength of my heart and my portion forever.

DEERFIELD.

"As the long train
Of ages glide away, the sons of men,
The youth in life's green spring, and he who goes
In the full strength of years, matron, and maid,
The bowed with age, the infant in the smiles
And beauty of its innocent age cut off,—
Shall, one by one, be gathered to thy side,
By those, who in their turn shall follow them."—BRYANT.

[The first person buried in this Burying Ground.]

Here Lyes ye Body of
JOSEPH BARNARD, Aged
45 years, Dec. September y^e
6th, 1695.

LIMON BEAMON,
Died 170½, aged 54.

Here Lyes y^e Body of
HANNAH BEAMON,
who departed this Lif y^e 13th of May, 1739,
in ye 94th year of her age.

M. A. DyED
NOVEM.   7,
ANNO   1696.

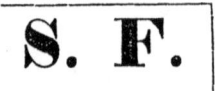

Here lies buried the Body of
Lievt. Mehuman Hinsdale,
who died May y^e 9th, 1736,
in the 63d year of his age.

Who was the first male child born in this place, and was twice
captivated by the Indian Salvages.

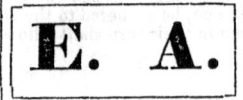

In memory of
Col°. Ephraim Williams, Esq.,
of Stockbridge, who died August y^e 11th, 1754,
in the 63d year of his age.

Blest be that hand divine which gently laid
My heart at rest beneath this humble shed.

Note.—The above was father of Col. Ephraim Williams, founder of Williams College.

In Memory of
Thomas Williams, Esq.,
who died Sept. 28, 1775, Æt 57.

To each unthinking being, heaven, a friend,
Gives not the useless knowledge of its end,
To man imparts it, but with such a view,
As while he dreads it makes him hope it too.

Here lies yᵉ Body of
the Rev'd Mr. John Williams,
the beloved and faithful Pastor of this place,
who dyed on June yᵉ 12th, 1729,
in the 65th year of his age.
Rev. 14, 13.
"Write, Blessed are ye dead who die in the Lord."

In memory of
Col. John Hawks,
who died June 24, 1784, in the 77th year of his age.
To be pure without superstition, faithful to our trust, pleasant in
our circle, and friendly to the poor, is to imitate his example.

In memory of
Mrs. Elizabeth,
Wife of John Hawks,
who died Feb. 28, 1799, aged 66.
Her children arise up and call her blessed.
Pray kind reader lend an ear,
As you are now so once was I,
As I am now so you must be,
Prepare for death and follow me.

Here lyeth the Body of
Mrs. Eunice Williams,
the virtuous and desirable consort of
the Rev. John Williams,
and daughter of Rev. Eleazer and Mrs. Esther Mather,
of Northampton.
She was born Aug. 2, 1664,
and fell by the rage of the barbarous enemy,
March 1, 1703⁴.
Prov. xxxi: 28. "Her children rise up and call her blessed."

Here lies interred the Body of
Mrs. Abigail Williams,
the relict of the Rev. Mr. John Williams, of this place.
She died June yᵉ 27th, 1754,
in the 82d year of her age.

Here lies the remains of
Mr. JUSTIN BULL,
who died June 5th, 1795, aged 61 years.
Tender were his feelings,
The christian was his friend,
Honest were his dealings,
And happy was his end.

In memory of
Mrs. HANNAH,
Wife of Mr. Samuel Dickinson,
who was drowned Sept. 3d, 1740,
in the 36th year of her age.

And HEBZIBAH,
Daughter of Mr. Samuel and Mrs. Hannah Dickinson,
who was drowned Sept. 3d, 1740,
in the 8th year of her age.
Life glows and smiles with prospects bright,
Our life is doomed to care and toil,
Old age, the lonely eve of night,
Quick death writes vanity on all.

Here lies Buried the Body of
DOCT. THOMAS WELLS,
who departed this life March the 7th, Anno Dom. 1713,
in the 59th year of his age.

NOTE. THIS is the oldest town in Franklin County; the Indian name was POCUMTUCK. A deed was made to John Pynchon, Esq., of Springfield, "for the use and behoof of major Eleazur Lusher, ensign Daniel Fisher, and other English at Dedham, their associates and successors," by *Chauk* alias *Chaque*, the sachem of Pocumtuck, and his brother *Wapahoale*, and is dated Feb. 24, 1665, prior to the grant by government. The deed is witnessed by *Wequonock*, who, " helped the Sachem in making the bargain ;" and reserves to the Indians " the right of fishing in the rivers and waters ; hunting deer, or other wild animals ; the gathering of walnuts, chestnuts, and other nuts, and things on the commons." The first settlement at Deerfield commenced in 1760, and within four years a considerable number of buildings were erected. In 1686, the Rev. John Williams was settled as minister of the place, on a salary of £60, to be paid in wheat at three shillings and three-pence the bushel, peas at two shillings and six-pence, Indian corn at two shillings, and salted pork at two-pence halfpenny the pound.

BATTLE MONUMENT AT BLOODY BROOK.

Erected August, 1831. On this ground Captain Thomas Lathrop, and Eighty-Four Men under his command, including Eighteen teamsters from Deerfield, Conveying Stores from that town to Hadley, were ambuscaded by about 700 Indians, and the Captain and Seventy-six Men Slain, September 18th 1765, (old Style). The Soldiers who fell, were described by a Cotemporary Historian as a Choice Company of Young Men, the very flower of the County of Essex. None of whom were ashamed to Speak with the enemy in the gate.
—"And SANGUINETTO tells you" where the dead "Made the earth wet and turned" the unwilling Waters Red.—

The grave of the Slain is Marked by a Stone Slab 21 Rods Southerly of this Monument.

GRAVE
OF
CAPT. LATHROP,
AND
MEN SLAIN
BY THE
INDIANS
1675.

This monument stands 30 or 40 rods southerly from the Congretional church. South-easterly from the monument is seen *Sugar-loaf Mountain*, a conical peak of red sand stone, about 650 feet in height. In 1835, the 160th anniversary of the destruction of Capt. Lathrop and his men was commemorated in this place. The Hon. Edward Everett, governor of Massachusetts, was appointed orator for the occasion, and General Epaphras Hoyt, of Deerfield, was appointed to make the address at the laying of the corner stone for the monument. About six thousand persons were present on this occasion. Governor Everett delivered his address under a walnut tree. About forty years after Capt. Lathrop and his men were killed, a rude monument was erected to their memory, but the different occupants of the soil removed it so many times, that it was a matter of uncertainty where he or his men were buried. In 1835, the committee of investigation, guided by the tradition of some aged people, found the spot where he and about thirty of his men were interred ; the grave was just in front of the dooryard of Stephen Whitney, Esq., and about twenty feet northwest of his front door. Their bones were in a state of tolerable preservation, but fell to pieces on exposure to the air. " A grave probably containing the bones of the ninety-six Indians who were slain on that day, was likewise found by accident about the same time, nearly one hundred rods west of the road leading from Bloody Brook to Conway, by Mr. Artemas Williams, and a little more than half a mile south-west of the grave of Lathrop."

The monument is six feet square and about twenty feet in height ; it is constructed of marble, by Mr. Woods of Sunderland. On its completion an address was delivered at its foot by Mr. Luther B. Lincoln, of Deerfield.

" For the distance of about three miles, after leaving Deerfield meadow, Lathrop's march lay through a very level country, closely wooded, where he was every moment exposed to an attack on either flank ; at the termination of this distance, near the south point of *Sugar-loaf Hill*, the road approximated Connecticut river, and the left was in some measure protected. At the village now called *Muddy Brook*, in the southerly part of Deerfield, the road crossed a small stream, bordered by a narrow morass, from which the village has its name ; though more appropriately it should be denominated *Bloody Brook*, by which it was sometimes known. Before arriving at the point of intersection with the brook, the road for about half a mile ran parallel with the morass, then, crossing, it continued directly to the south point of Sugar-loaf Hill, traversing what is now the home lots, on the east side of the village. As the morass was thickly covered with brush, the place of crossing afforded a favorable point of surprise. On discovering Lathrop's march, a body of upwards of seven hundred Indians planted themselves in ambuscade at this point, and lay eagerly waiting to pounce upon him while passing the morass. Without scouring the woods in his front and flanks, or suspecting the snare laid for him, Lathrop arrived at the fatal spot; crossed the morass with the principal part of his force, and probably halted, to allow time for his teams to drag through their loads. The critical moment had arrived—the Indians instantly poured a heavy and destructive fire upon the column, and rushed furiously to close attack. Confusion and dismay succeeded. The troops broke and scattered, fiercely pursued by the Indians, whose great superiority enabled them to attack at all points. Hopeless was the situation of the scattered troops, and they resolved to sell their lives in a vigorous struggle. Covering themselves with trees, the bloody conflict now became a severe trial of skill in sharp shooting, in which life was the *stake*. Difficult would it be to describe the havoc, barbarity, and misery that ensued; 'fury raged, and shuddering pity quit the sanguine field,' while desperation stood pitted, at 'fearful odds,' to unrelenting ferocity. The dead, the dying, the wounded, strewed the ground in all directions; and Lathrop's devoted force was soon reduced to a small number, and resistance became faint. At length the unequal struggle terminated in the annihilation of nearly the whole of the English; only seven or eight escaped from the bloody scene, to relate the dismal tale; and the wounded were indiscriminately butchered. Capt. Lathrop fell in the early part of the action. The whole loss, including teamsters, amounted to ninety.

Capt. Mosely, who was at Deerfield with his company, between four and five miles distance, hearing the musketry, hurried on to the relief of Lathrop, but it was too late; he found the Indians had done their bloody work, and were stirpping the dead. Rushing on in close order, he broke through the enemy, and, charging back and forth, cut down all within the range of his shot. After several hours of gallant fighting, the savages were compelled to seek for safety in the surrounding swamps and forests. Lieutenants Savage and Pickering greatly distinguished themselves by their skill and bravery. Just at the close of the action, Major Treat, of Connecticut, who on the morning of this day had marched towards Northfield, arrived on the ground with one hundred men, consisting of English, Pequot and Mohegan Indians, and shared in the final pursuit of the enemy. Capt. Mosely lost but two men in the various attacks, and seven or eight only were wounded. The loss of the Indians in the various attacks of the day was estimated at ninety-six, the greatest proportion of which fell in the engagement with Mosely. On the approach of night, Treat and Mosely proceeded to Deerfield, where they encamped for the night, and the next morning returned to the field of slaughter to bury the dead. The day after this disaster, the Indians appeared at Deerfield, on the west side of the river in that town, and, displaying the garments they had stripped from Lathrop's slain, made demonstrations of an attack on the fortified house, which then contained a garrison of only twenty-seven men. The commander held out delusive appearances of a strong force,— caused his trumpet signals to be given, as if to call in additional troops, which so intimidated the Indians that they withdrew without making an attack. This post, however, was afterwards abandoned by the garrison, and the place was soon after destroyed by the enemy.

GREENFIELD.

"Oh, all unshaken
Is the cold, deep spell around them,
Pulseless every breast;
In the slumber that hath bound them,
They must ever rest.

Bright, pure ones taken
From the earth so glad and blooming,
From life's treacherous wave,
While rich flowers the air perfuming,
Nod above their grave."—D. ELLEN GOODMAN.

[The Oldest Monument.]
In Memory of
EDWARD ALLIN,
who died Dec. 10, 1756, in ye 69 year of his age.
"Blessed are the dead who die in the Lord." Rev. xxx.

OBED,
Son of Mr. Ebenezer and Mrs. Elisabeth Wells,
Died Sept. 10th, 1758,
aged 11 years and 7 months.

In memory of
Mr. JOEL GRAVES,
who died April y⁰ 16, A. D. 1760, aged 23 years.

In memory of
Mr. ASA WELLS,
who died Nov. y⁰ 7th, 1761, A. D.,
in the 32 year of his age.

[The Oldest Monument in the North Burying Ground.]
In memory of
Mrs. SEBRA,
Wife of Capt. Isaac Newton,
who died Dec'r y⁰ 25th, 1775,
in y⁰ 25th year of her age.

In Memory of
Mrs. REBECKAH HINSDALE,
the virtuous and amiable Consort of
Mr. Samuel Hinsdale,
who died Augst 16th, 1760,
in y⁰ 48th year of her age.
" A virtuous woman is a crown to her husband."
"Death is a debt to nature due;
Which I have paid, and so must you."

REV. ROGER NEWTON, D. D.,
was ordained to the Gospel Ministry in
this town, 18 Nov. 1761,
and died 10 December, 1816,
in the 80 year of his age, and 56 of his Ministry.
His life was adorned with private and domestic virtues, and distinguished by publick and professional usefulness.

Mrs. MARY NEWCOMB,
Wife of R. E. Newcomb, Esq.,
and last surviving child of Gen. Joseph Warren,
who fell on Bunker Hill, June 17, 1775,
Died Feb. 9, 1826, Æ 54.

MONTAGUE.

In memory of
Mr. Elijah Bardwell,
who died Jan'y 26, 1786, in yᵉ 27th year of his age.

Having but a few days survived ye fatal night, when he was flung from his horse, and drawn by ye stirrups 26 rods along ye path, as appeared by the place where his hat was found, and here he had spent ye whole of the following severe cold night, treading down the snow in a small circle. The family he left was an aged father, a wife, and three small children.

BERNARDSTON.

In memory of
the Hon. Major John Burke,
who died Oct. 27, 1784,
in yᵉ Sixty-Seventh year of his age.

" Were I so tall to reach the pole,
 Or grasp the ocean with my span,
I must be measured by my soul,—
 The mind's the standard of the man."

BELCHERTOWN.

Sacred to the memory of
Rev. Justus Forward,
Pastor of the Church in Belchertown,
Who, skilled in Evangelical Doctrine, exemplary in Christian duty, prudent in council, valiant for the truth, faithful and successful in labors, after a long and useful ministry, in which with reputation to himself, and to the spiritual benefit of his flock, he served God, and his generation, fell asleep March 8, A. D. 1814, in the 84th year of his age, and the 59th of his ministry. "Blessed are the dead who die in the Lord."

VERNON, VERMONT.

[The Oldest Monument in this Burying Ground.]

Here lies cut down like unripe fruit,
A Son of Mr. AMOS TuTE,
And of MRS. JEMiME TuTE his Wife,
Called JONATHAN; of whose frail life,

The days all summed how short the account,
Scarcely to fourteen years amount,
Born the 12th of May was he,
In Seventeen Hundred Sixty-Three ;

To death he fell a helpless Prey,
On April V & Twentieth day,
In Seventeen Hundred Seventy-Seven,
Quiting this world we hope for Heaven.

Behold the amazing alteration,
Effected by —— innoculation,
The means employed his Life to save,
Hurried him headlong to the grave.

Full in the bloom of youth he fell,
Alas what human tongue can tell,
The *Mother's* grief, her anguish show,
Or paint the *Father's* heavier woe.

Who now no Natral offspring has
His ample fortune —— to possess,
To fill his place Stand in his stead,
Or bear his name when he is dead.

So God ordand, His ways are just,
Tho' Empires Crumble into dust;
Life and the world mere bubles are,
Let loos to these, for Heaven prepare.

NOTE.—The above was written by REV. BUNKER GAY, an eccentric Minister of this town.

SARAH NEWELL,
Wife of George Semour, Daughter of
Arad and Sarah Hunt, Born May 7, 1821,
Died at Litchfield, Ct., April 21, 1843.

"Not lost, but gone before."

In memory of
Mrs. MARTHA BRIDGMAN,
Wife of Capt. Orlando Bridgman,
who died April ye 3d, 1766, in the 68th year of her age,
and the first person that was buried in this yard.

Sacred to the memory of
CAPT. ORLANDO BRIDGMAN,
who departed this life
June 4th, 1771, in the 70th year of his age.

"Whilst living men my tomb do view,
Remember well here's room for you."

THE HON.
JOHN BRIDGMAN, ESQ.,
A MAN of splendid abilities and eminent
usefulness in his day,
An implacable enemy of Vice, Superstition and
Bigotry, and ardent lover and friend of
Virtue and Religion,
Cheerful in Prosperity, in Adversity Placid & Submissive.
Christian Piety and Morality, Probity and
Fidelity, Justice, Temperance
Humility, Industry & good economy adorn'd his LIF.
Ob. FEB 26, 1805, Æt 68.

"The upright man whose end is peace,
Dying, obtain'd a sweet release;
And when the just to life shall rise,
Among the first he'll mount the skies."

Memento Mori.

Sacred to the Memory of
Mrs. RUTH BRIDGMAN,
Consort of John Bridgman, Esq.,
who died June 1, 1797, in the 58th year of her age.

Behold and see as you pass by,
As you are now so once was I,
As I am now you soon must be,
Prepare for death, and follow me.

The unfortunate
MIRANDA,
Daughter of John & Ruth Bridgman,
whose remains are here interred, fell a prey to the
flames that consomd her Father's Hoose,
on ye 11th of June, 1791, aged 28.

The room below flamed like a stove,
Anxious for those who slept above,
She ventured on ye trembling floor,
It fell, she sank and rose no more.

In memory of
Mr. Amos Tute,
who died April 17th, 1790, in the 60th year of his age.
"Were I so tall to reach the pole,
Or grasp the ocean with my span,
I must be measured by my soul,
The mind's the standard of the man."

Mrs. Jemima Tute,
Successively Relict of Messrs.
William Phips, Caleb Howe & Amos Tute.
The two first were killed by the Indians,
Phips, July 5th, 1743, Howe, June 27th, 1755.
When Howe was killed she and her Children, then seven in number, were carried into captivity. The oldest daughter went to France, and was married to a French Gentleman. The youngest was torn from her breast, and perished with hunger. By the aid of some benevolent Gent'n, and her own personal heroism, she recovered the rest. She had two by her last husband, outlived both him and them, and died March 7th, 1805, having passed through more vicissitudes, and endured more hardships, than any of her cotemporaries.
"No more can Savage foe annoy,
Nor aught her wide spread fame destroy."

Here lies the Body of
Mr. James Tute,
who departed — this life April — the — 14th, 1775,
aged — about 90 years.
"When living men my tomb do view,
Remember well here's room for you."

HON. JONATHAN HUNT,
Born in Northfield, Mass., September 23, 1738,
Died in Vernon, June 1, 1823, aged 85.

Susannah,
Widow of Hon. Jonathan Hunt,
Died June 29, 1834, Æ 85.

GEN. ARAD HUNT,
Died Feb 18, 1825, in his 82 year.

Arad Hunt,	Sally Hunt,
Died	wife of Arad Hunt,
Aug. 30, 1833,	Died Sept. 15, 1846,
aged 43.	aged 52.

GUILFORD, VT.

Sacred to the memory of the
Hon. BENJAMIN CARPENTER, Esq ,
Born in Rehobath, Mass., A. D. 1726,
A Magistrate in Rhode Island in 1794,
A Public Teacher of Righteousness,
An able advocate to his last for Democracy,
and the equal rights of man,
Removed to this town A. D. 1870,
Was a Field Officer in the Revolutionary War,
A founder of the first Constitution and
Government of Vermont,
A Counsellor of Errors in A. D. 1783,
A member of the Council, and Lieut. Governor of the
State in A. D. 1779,
A firm professor of Christianity in the Baptist Church
fifty years, left this world,
And 146 persons of lineal posterity, March 29th, 1804,
Aged 78 years 10 months and 12 days,
With a strong mind, and full faith of
a more glorious state hereafter.
Statue about six feet — weight 200lbs.
Death had no terror.

WESTMINSTER, VT.

In memory of
WILLIAM FRENCH,
Son of Mr. Nathaniel French,
who was shot at Westminster, March ye 13, 1775,
by the hands of cruel Ministerial Tools of George ye 3d,
in the Cort house, at a 11 a'clock at night,
in the 22d year of his age.

> Here William French his Body lies,
> For Murder, his Blood for Vengeance cries,
> King George the Third his Tory Crew,
> Tha wich a bawl his head Shot threw,
> For Liberty and his Country's Good
> Lost his Life, his Dearest blood.

Sacred to the memory of
CAPTAIN THOMAS FORRIST,
late of London, in the Kingdom of Great Britain,
who died on the 20th day of May, A. D. 1795,
aged 67.

After a long and laborious life, spent chiefly in the service of the English East India Company, in exploring the dangerous, unknown navigation of the Mollucca and Philippine Islands, the Coast of New Guinea, and other parts of the Indian Seas, no less amiable in private, than active in public life. His death was sincerely regreted by all who knew him, as a loss to his friends in particular, and to society at large.

EPITAPHS.

In memory of
Mrs. HANNAH MCNEIL,
Relict of Mr. Nehemiah McNeil,
who died June the 6th, 1795, aged 75 years.

> Attend ye people to God's Laws,
> And strictly lend an ear,
> The words that from my dust procede
> Attentively do hear.
> O, world of people praise the Lord,
> For bountiful is he,
> His tender mercies doth endure
> To all eternity.

Vitæ Summa brevis spem nos vetat inchoare longam.

To perpetuate the memory of
Mrs. GRATIA BRADLEY,
the amiable consort of the Hon. Stephen R. Bradley,
Member of the Senate of the United States,
who died the 10th day of January,
in the Year of Redemption 1802,
and of her age the 34th.

Mrs. MERAB BRADLEY,
the early wife and affectionate friend of
Stephen R. Bradley, Esq.,
who departed this life on the 7th day of April,
in the year of our Lord 1785,
in the 28th year of her age.

Accept, departed friends, the last tribute of affection which your deserted and disconsolate partner can bestow. His last hope will be to rest from his sorrows beside you, or to dwell with you in the habitation "made without hands, eternal in the heavens," then perhaps when "there shall be none to mourn," some stranger who has known and felt the loss of those virtues which adorn the Wife, the Mother, the Sister and the Friend, will pause and drop a tear over the ashes in which they once resided.

> Insatiate archer! could not one suffice?
> Thy shaft flew twice, and twice my peace was slain.

Azubah,
Wife of Aaron Hitchcock,
Born Jan. 18, 1795, married Jan. 21, 1827,
Died Jan. 7, 1842.

Elizabeth,
Wife of Rev. Wm. H. Gilbert,
Died Dec. 13, 1846, Æ 25.
I opened not my mouth because thou did'st it.

BRATTLEBORO', VT.

Erected in memory of
Mrs. Mercy Whitney,
Consort of Doct' Ephraim Whitney,
who died Feb'y 26th, A. D. 1792,
aged 50 years.
"While the dear dust she leaves behind,
Sleeps in thy bosom, sacred tomb,
Soft be her bed, her slumber kind,
And all her dreams, of joys to come."

This is in memory of
Mr. Timothy Whipple,
who departed this life November 4th, 1796,
in the 72d year of his age.
"Deliriums State, was worse than fate;
And vacancy of mind;
But real grace, fill'd up the space,
And left a hope behind."

This stone consecrated to the memory of
MADAM JANE ROBBINS,
Consort of the late Rev. Doc. Robbins,
who languished from his death, 30 June, 1799,
till 12 Sept. Anno Domini, 1800, when, in the 60 year of
her age, she commenced her inseparable union
with her much beloved consort, and her tombstone is
erected by the piety of her afflicted children.

NEWBURYPORT.

"This Cenotaph
Is erected with affectionate
veneration, to
The memory of the
Rev. GEORGE WHITFIELD,
Born at Gloucester, England,
December 16, 1714.
Educated at Oxford University;
Ordained 1736.
In a ministry of thirty-four years,
He crossed the Atlantic thirteen times,
And preached more
Than eighteen thousand sermons.
As a soldier of the
Cross, humble, devout, ardent,
He put on the
Whole armour of God; preferring
The honor of Christ
To his own interest, repose,
Reputation, and life.

CONCORD.

God wills us free; man wills us slaves. I will as God wills, God's will be done.
Here lies the body of
JOHN JACK,
a native of Africa,
who died March, 1773, aged about 60 years.
Though born in a land of slavery, he was born free; though he lived in a land of liberty, he lived a slave, till, by his honest, though stolen labours, he acquired the source of slavery, which gave him his freedom, though not long before death, the grand tyrant, gave him his final emancipation, and set him on a footing with kings. Though a slave to vice, he practiced those virtues, without which, kings are but slaves.

NOTE.—This was written by Daniel Bliss, Esq.

DORCHESTER.

Hear lyes our Captaine, & MAJOR of Suffolk was withall,
A godley Magistrate was he, and MAJOR GENERALL
Two Troops of hors with him here Came,
Such worth his love did Crave ;
Ten Companyes of Foot also Mourning Marcht to his grave.
Let all that read be sure to keep the faith as he has don,
With Christ he lives now crown'd,
His name was HUMPHREY ATHERTON
He dyed the 16 of September 1661.

PLYMOUTH.

The Pilgrim Fathers where are they?
  The waves that brought them o'er
Still roll in the bay and throw their spray,
  As they break along the shore
Still roll in the bay as they rolled that day,
  When the May-Flower moored below ;
When the sea around was black with storms,
  And white the shore with snow.

The Pilgrim Fathers are at rest,
  When Summer's throned on high,
And the world's warm breast is in verdure dress'd,
  Go stand on the hill where they lie.
The earliest ray of the golden day
  On that hallowed spot is cast;
And the evening sun as he leaves the world,
  Looks kindly on that spot last."—PIERPONT.

The most ancient Inscriptions are on Burying Hill, formerly *Fort Hill*, it is in the rear of the Town rising one hundred and sixty-five feet above the Sea-level, embracing about eight acres, on the summit of the south-west side, the PILGRIMS erected first some temporary defence, but on the approach of Phillip's war they erected a strong fort one hundred feet square, strongly palisadoed, ten and a half feet high; no other place could have been so well chosen either for discovering the approach of Savages, or for defending the town against their attacks ; it is covered with the symbols of mortality; the sepulchres of our PILGRIM FATHERS. Here we tread on the ashes of those to whom we are indebted under providence for our most precious earthly enjoyments, Religious and Civil liberty.

Here lies the body of
EDWARD GRAY, Gent.
aged about 52 years,
and departed this life about the last of June 1681.

Departed this life, 23 June, 1796,
in the 90 year of her age,
MADAM PRISCILLA HOBART,
relict of the Rev. Noah Hobart, late of Fairfield,
in Connecticut, her third husband.
Her first and second were
John Watson, Esq , and Hon. Isaac Lothrop.

In memory of
DOCTOR LAZARUS LE BARON,
who departed this life,
2 September, 1773, æt. suæ 75.

My flesh shall slumber in the ground
Till the last trumpet's joyful sound;
Then burst the chains, with sweet surprise,
And in my Saviour's likeness rise.

Here lyeth buried the body of
that precious servant of God
MR. THOMAS CUSHMAN,
who, after he had served his generation
according to the will of God, and particularly
the Church of Plymouth, for many years, in the office of
a ruling elder, fell asleep in Jesus, 10 Dec. 1691,
and in the 84 year of his age.

ANDREW FARRELL,
of respectable connections, in Ireland,
aged 38 years,
owner and commander of the ship, Hibernia,
sailed from Boston, 26 Jan. and was wrecked on Plymouth beach, 28 Jan. 1805.
His remains with five of seven seamen,
who perished with him, are here interred.

O piteous lot of man's uncertain state;
What woes on life's eventful journey wait!
By sea, what treacherous calms, what sudden storms,
And death, attendant in a thousand forms!

EPITAPHS.

Here Lyes yͤ Body of yͤ
Honorable Major WILLIAM BRADFORD,
who expired February yͤ 20 1703-4
aged 79 years.

"He lived long, but still was doing good,
And in his country's service lost much blood.
After a life well spent, he's now at rest,—
His very name and memory is blest."

Here lies buried the body of
MR. THOMAS CLARK,
aged 98 years, who departed this life,
the 24 of March, 1697.

This stone is erected to the
memory of that unbiassed judge, faithful officer,
sincere friend, and honest man,
COL. ISAAC LOTHROP,
who resigned this life, on the 26 day of April, 1750,
in the 43 year of his age.

Had virtue's charms the power to save
Its faithful votaries from the grave,
This stone had ne'er possess'd the fame
Of being mark'd with Lothrop's name.

In memory of
GEORGE WATSON, ESQ.,
who died the 3d of Dec. 1800,
in the 33 year of his age.

No folly wasted his paternal store,
No guilt, no sordid av'rice made it more.
With honest fame and sober plenty crown'd,
He liv'd and spread his cheering influence round.
Pure was his walk and peaceful was his end
We bless'd his rev'rend length of days,
And hail'd him, in the publick ways,
With veneration and with praise,
Our father and our friend.

To the memory of
John Cotton, Esq.
formerly a minister of the gospel at Halifax,
which employ was ever his greatest delight,
who died, 4 Nov. A. D. 1789,
in the 78 year of his age.

Tis heaven's irrevocable decree,
That the great, the good, the pious shall fall,
In that dark grave undistinguish'd to lie,
Till the last trumpet rends the azure sky;
When the virtuous immortal will rise,
To glory and joys, above the starry skies;
The vitious to pain, dishonor, contempt,
In realms, below the splendid firmament.

DANVERS.

This humble stone in memory of
Elizabeth Whitman,
is inscribed by her weeping Friends.

To whom she endeared herself by uncommon tenderness and affection. Endowed with superior genius and acquirements, she was still more endeared by humility and benevolence. Let candor throw a veil over, for great was her Charity for others. She sustained the last painful scene far from every friend, and exhibited an example of calm resignation. Her departure was on the 25th of July. A. D. 1788, in the 37th year of her age. And the tears of Strangers watered her grave.

Note. She was better known to readers of romance by the name of "Eliza Wharton."

EAST HARTFORD, CONN.

[The oldest Monument in East Hartford is about two feet square, a few rods north of Gov. Pitkin's Table Monument, and is in a good state of preservation. On it is the following inscription:]

HERE LIETH THE BO
Dy OF ObADi
AH WOOD WHO
DIED APRIL THE
11, 1712, in the
64 yEAR oF
HIS AGE.

In Memory of
Mr. PHIÑEAS,
Son of Mr. Thomas and Mrs Mary Burnham,
who died tryumphingly,
in hops of a goyful resurection
in Dec. y° 22nd, A. D. 1776,
in y° 23d year of his age.

Here lies the
REV'D ELIPHALET WILLIAMS, D. D.,
who died June 29, 1803,
in the 77th year of his age, and 56th of his ministry.
He was an able orthodox, faithful, Laborious, Exemplary & Successful Minister of Jesus Christ, patient under long and sharp bodily distress, Resigned to the will of his Master, He committed himself to Him that judgeth righteously. "Blessed are the dead who die in the Lord."

EPITAPHS.

Here lieth interred the body of
the Honorable William Pitkin, Esqr.,
late Governor of the Colony of Connecticut,
To the God of Nature indebted for all his Talents,
for which Glory he aimed to Imploy them ;
In Religion without affectation,
Chearfull, Humble and Temperate,
Zealous and bold for the Truth,
Faithfull in Distributing Justice,
Scattering away Evil with his Eye,
an Example of Christian Virtues,
A Patron of his Country,
A Benefactor to the Poor,
A Tender Parent & Faithfull Friend.
Twelve Years he presided in the Superior Court,
and three Years and an half Governor in Chief,
after Serving his Generation, by the Will of God,
with Calmness and serenity, fell on Sleep
the 1st day of October, A. D. 1769,
in the 76 year of his age.

Walk Thoughtfull on the Solemn Shore
Of that Vast Ocean thou art Soon to pass.

Here lyes Interr'd the Body of
the Rev'd M^R. Sam^{LL} Woodbridge,
who haveing for about forty years fulfilled his
Ministry in the 3rd C^{hh} of Christ in Hartford,
Fell asleep June the 9th, 1746,
in the 63d year of his age.

Here lies interred the Body of
Mrs. Content Woodbridge,
the late pious & Virtuous Consort, of the
Rev'd Mr. Samuel Woodbridge,
Who fell asleep July ye 28th, A. D. 1758,
In ye 67 year of her age.
She was an Ornament to Religion in the Different
Stations She Sustained.

In Memory of
Mrs MARY,
Wife of Mr. John Fowler,
who departed this life April ye 3d, 1776,
in ye 39th year of her age.
"Another hear lies, not alone,
For she's three daughters near this stone."

In Memory of
JERRYMY R. WILLIAMS,
who was killed by lightning, Aug. 27, 1809,
aged 27 years.

Here Lyes ye Body of
MARY,
ye wife of Daniel Deckanson,
her maiden name was Mary Williamson,
Deceased April ye 6th, 1718,
in ye 30th year of her age.
Her child lyes by her right side.

Under this Monument lies interred
ye remains of JONATHAN HILLS, ESQ.,
who departed this life Feb. ye 22d, A. D. 1775,
in ye 78th year of his age.
"Hope humbly then, with humble pinions soar;
Wait the great Teacher death, and God adore."

CAPT. JOSEPH MERRIMAN,
was lost at Sea, 1834, aged 44.

EUNICE,
his wife, died Sept. 15, 1849.

Sacred to the memory of
WILLIAM H. DRAKE,
who was born in New York, Dec. 9, 1813,
died June 12th, 1847.

In Memory of
DEACON JOHN GOODWIN,
who departed this life Sept. the 14th, 1793,
aged 87 years.

"Life is unsertain, death is sure,
Sin is the wound, and Christ the cure."

Here lies ye precious dust
of that desireable woman,
Mrs. MARY WILLIAMS,
Consort of ye Rev. Eliph Williams,
Courteous, Benevolent and Pious, a pattern of Conjugal and Parental affection, a rich blessing to her family; how rich this Stone han't power to tell. She departed this life in hope of a better, June 28th, 1776, in ye 50th year of her age. "Go Reader, Love thy Soul, and Learn to die."

In Memory of
Mr. JONATHAN BURR,
Died at Mr. Elisha Burr's Feb. ye 9th, 1770,
in ye 78th year of his age.

WINDSOR, CONN.

Here lyeth the body of
the HON. ROGER WOLCOTT, ESQ.,
of Windsor, who for several years was
Governor of the Colony of Connecticut,
died May 17th, Anno Ætatis 89, Salutis 1767.

Earths highest station ends in here he lies,
And dust to dust concludes her noblest song.

NEW HAVEN, CONN.

J. D. Esq.
deceased March ye 18th,
in ye 82d year of his age, 1688-9

NOTE.—This is a copy of the inscription on the headstone of John Dixwell, one of the regicides, who fled to this country on the restoration of king Charles, the second.—[*See Stiles' Hist. Regicides.*]

In memory of the
Hon. ROGER SHERMAN,
mayor of the city of New Haven,
and senator of the United States.
He was born at Newton, in Massachusetts, 19 April 1721, and died at New Haven 23 July, A. D. 1793, aged 72.
Possessed of a strong, clear, and penetrating mind, and singular perseverence, he became the self taught scholar. Eminent for jurisprudence and policy, he was nineteen years an assistant, and twenty-three years a judge of the supreme court in high reputation. He was a delegate in the first congress, signed the glorious act of independence, and many years displayed superior talents and ability in the national legislature. He was a member of the general convention, approved the federal constitution, and served his country with fidelity and honour in the house of representatives, and in the senate of the United States. He was a man of improved integrity, a cool discerning judge, a prudent sagacious politician, a true, faithful, and firm patriot. He ever adorned the profession of christianity, which he made in youth, and was distinguished through life for public usefulness, and died in the prospect of a blessed immortality.

WM. JONES, Esq. Dep. Gov.
dec. 17 Oct. 1706, ætat. 82.

Mrs. HANNAH JONES,
dec. 4 May, 1707, ætat. 74.

The memory of the just is blessed.

THEOPHILUS EATON, Esq. GOV.
dec. 7 Jan. 1657, ætat. 67.

EATON so famed, so wise, so meek, so just;
The phœnix of our world, here hides his dust,
This name forget N. England never must.
To attend you, syr, undr these framed stones,
Are come yor hond son and daughter Jones,
On each hand to repose yr weary bones.

Here lyeth interred the body of the
Reverend and Learned Mr. THOMAS CLAP,
the late president of Yale College, in New Haven.

A truly great man, a gentleman of superior natural genius, most assiduous application, and indefatigable industry. In the various branches of learning he greatly excelled; an accomplished instructor; a patron of the college; a great divine; bold for the truth; a zealous promoter and defender of the doctrines of grace; of unaffected piety, and a pattern of every virtue, the tenderest of fathers and best of friends, the glory of learning, and an ornament of religion; for thirteen years, the faithful and much respected pastor of the church in Windham; and, near 27 years, the laborious and faithful president of the college, and having served his own generation, by the will of God, with serenity and calmness, he fell on sleep, the 7 day of January, 1767 in his 64 year.

Death, great proprietor of all,
'Tis thine to tread out empires
And to quench the stars.

In memory of
Captain ROBERT TOWNSEND,
who departed this life,
19 Nov. 1806, in the 59 year of his age.

This spot contains the ashes of the just,
Who sought no honours and betray'd no trust.
This truth he prov'd, in every path he trod,
An honest man's the noblest work of God.

INDEX.

	Page.		Page.
Allen, Ellen W.	70	Adams, Eliza P.	103
William	70	David	103
Charles R.	70	Mary E.	103
Dea'n Samuel	17	David	103
Phineas	40	Sarah P.	103
Jonathan	40	Bancroft, Sarah H.	128
Maj.	40	Burt, Eben	22
Joseph	41	Henry	14
Elizabeth	41	Bartlett, Samvel	16
Elisha	41	Sarah	16
H. Maria	41	Joseph	86
William Esq.	41	Benjamin	86
Elijah	41	Bradford, Hon. William	203
Keziah	41	Bagg, David	140
Sarah J. B.	70	Bontecou, Sibyl	127
Ashmun, Eli P.	56	Beck, Louisa A.	72
Lucy	56	Bolter, William	65
Sophia W.	57	Bascom, Joseph	19
Orpha	57	Brown, Rev. John	134
Mary C.	128	Bull, Justin	184
Sarah H.	128	Barnard, Joseph	181
Ashley, Benjamin	139	Brooks, Joanna	126
Elenor	142	Barnard, Abner	31
Joseph	142	Rachel	30
John	154	Abner	83
Alvord Ben'n	56	Barrett, Rebecca	103
A. M.	181	Byers, Sophia	114
A. E.	182	Capt. James	114
Alexander Nathaniel	19	Hannah	114
John	27	Bryant John	114
Sarah	27	Hannah M.	114
John	27	Henry K	115
Daniel	26	Frederick	115
Atkins, Zenas	155	Frederick	115
Abbott, Maria L.	96	Burt, Dea. Nathaniel	144
Atherton, Gen. Humphrey.	200	Solomon	144
Allin, Edward	188	Lieut. Nathaniel	145

INDEX.

	Page.
Berrya	100
Bond, Royal	123
Brainerd, David	36
Baker, Edward	35
Capt. John	46
Stephen	180
Capt. John	46
Rebeckah	46
Holister	105
Barber, Dea. John	136
Thomas	136
Breck, Joseph H.	93
Col. John	65
Electa	65
Clarissa	65
Theodore	66
Rev. Robert	116
Eunice	126
Fanny	92
Martin	92
William	93
Butler, Lewis	81
Mary A.	81
Edward	81
William	81
Mary	81
William	81
John B.	82
Daniel	82
Anna	82
Mary	82
Simeon	82
Rev. Amos	157
Abigail W.	86
Charles P.	86
Bliss, Abigail	130
Wid. Margaret	110
Samuel	110
Ebenezer	110
Jedediah	110
Rachel	110
Mariam	110
Alex	110
Margaret	111
Abigail	111
Edmund	111
Bliss, Alex	111
Margaret	111
Thomas W.	111
Richard	111
Thomas W.	111
Edmund	111
Elijah	111
Gen. Jacob	115
Col. John	115
Jacob Jun.	115
Emily	115
Lieut. Timothy	115
Doct. Jonathan	117
Doct. Pelatiah	117
Pelatiah	117
Hon. Moses	130
Brewer, Rev. Dan'el	117
Daniel Jun.	117
Katherine	118
Nathaniel	118
Eunice	118
Doct. Chauncy	118
Amy	118
Lucy	118
Kate	118
Charles	118
Anne	118
Belden, Rev. Pomeroy	169
Baldwin, Elnathan	147
Burnel, Hannah	179
Bishop, Eliza	152
Boltwood, Solomon	169
Lieut. Solomon	169
Ballantine, Rev. John	154
Ball, Rev. Nehemiah	154
Bryant, Benjamin	180
Bullard, Paul	161
Bridgman, James	101
Sarah	101
James	101
Sally M.	101
Henry	101
Joseph Cook	101
Capt. Orlando	192
Hon. John	193
Ruth	195

INDEX. 213

	Page.		Page.
Bridgman, Miranda	193	Clark, John P.	91
Thomas	101	Achsa	92
Thomas	102	A. M.	92
Thomas	102	Sylvester	99
Elizabeth	102	Church, Sylvia	100
William	102	Cook, Major Aaron	14
Betsey	102	Joseph	60
Bradley, Gratia	197	Dea. Noah	60
Merab	197	Elijah	60
Beamon, Limon	181	Abigail	60
Hannah	181	Capt. Joseph	59
Bardwell, Elijah	190	Justin	58
Bnrk, Maj. John	190	Capt. Joseph	55
Burnham, Phineas	205	Lydia	55
Burr, Jonathan	208	Emeline	61
Clarke, Lieut. William	13	Enos	61
Clark, Mercy	18	Hannah	61
Rachel	18	Capt'n Noah	162
Sam'l	23	Carpenter, Hon. Benjamin.	195
Rebecka	27	Cotton, John	204
Martha	28	Clark, William	93
Sarah	29	Jerusha	93
Dorcas	38	Mary	93
Martha	45	Lucius	93
Seth D.	60	Miranda	94
Lem'l C.	60	Sarah	94
Lemuel	59	Thomas	203
Lucretia	59	Cooley, Earl	121
Ezra	53	Curtis, Nathaniel	17
Martha	53	Samuel	90
Anna	51	Corse, Eben'r	164
Zeurah	61	Sarah	163
Charlotte	61	Chauncy, Rev. Isaac	135
William	67	Clap, Cap. Preserved	19
Josiah	67	Mehetable	20
Mary	67	Capt. Roger	30
Dea. Josiah	68	Suply	35
Sophia	69	Hannah	35
Eunice	160	Elizabeth	38
Rozel	160	Suply	52
Medad	160	Lucretia	53
Martha	88	Ezra	151
Lydia	91	Thomas	160
Lucinda	91	Maj'r Jonathan	163
Christopher	91	Cap. Luther	164
Elizabeth W.	91	Tirzah	164

214 INDEX.

	Page		Page
Clapp, Thomas Rev	210	Dwight, William H	85
Clap, Roger	165	Josiah	85
Anny	165	Thomas	85
Preserved	88	Dickanson, Mary	207
Sarah	88	Drake, William H	207
Eliphaz	88	Draper, Rev. Ichabod	168
Rachel	88	Dewey, Francis A	72
Cushman, Thomas	202	David L	76
Cooley Abigal	119	James C	96
Cole, Cyrus P	123	Edward J	96
Child, Ann	123	Henry C	96
William	123	Dickenson, Capt. James	73
Chapin, Abilene	110	Josiah	74
Japhat	110	Wealthy	74
Sarah	110	Seth H	74
John P	124	Caroline	74
Erastus S	124	Cotton	74
Francis N	124	Olive	74
Arabilla	125	Rev. Austin	170
Callender, M. C	123	Samuel F	170
Colton, Elizabeth	113	Lucretia G	170
Capt'n Thomas	144	Dea. Obadiah	173
Capt. Isaac	145	Hannah	184
Coleman, Doct. Seth	170	Hepzibah	184
Cutler, Doct. Robert	170	Day, Samuel	140
Doct. Isaac G	171	Major John	140
Doolittle, Rev. W. N	60	Mary	140
Dwit, Nathaniel	136	Drak, Mary	143
Dwight, Clarissa	56	Dyer, Benjamin	155
Caroline W	56	Drayton, Hannah	105
Margaretta	56	Dixon, Ruth	84
Francis H	55	Eaton, Theopilus Esq	210
Timothy E	55	Edwards, Eben	24
Sarah	112	Jonathan	36
Hon. Thomas	121	Jerusha	36
Hannah	121	Ebenezer	38
Hon. Jonathan	121	Lucy	38
Margaret	122	Mary	73
James S	122	Nathaniel	73
Mary S	122	Elizabeth	74
James S	122	Elisha	127
Jonathan	122	Frank	127
Hannah	122	Stanley	127
Thomas	128	Timothy	161
Sarah	129	Timothy	162
Timothy E	85	Ogden E	94

INDEX. 215

Name	Page
Edwards, Catherine	95
Mary S.	95
Thomas S.	95
Eugene	95
Pomeroy	95
Harriet	95
Eudns, Rebeccah	138
Ely, Ensign John	137
Dea. John	137
Mercy	137
Caleb	137
Samuel	137
Mary	138
Mary Wid.	138
Dorcas	138
Mary	139
Anna	139
Seth	139
Pamilia	139
Samuel	140
Major John	141
Edmund	153
Franklin	153
Flint, Hannah W.	77
F. S.	182
Fairfield, Abigal	21
Prvdence	21
Freedom, Susan	118
Foot, Adonijah	130
Adonijah	130
Fowler, Porter	152
Mary	207
Hon. Samuel	155
Jemima	155
Samuel	155
Farrell, Andrew	202
Fenner	95
Forward, Rev. Justice	191
French, William	196
Forrist, Capt. Thomas	196
E. G.	1
Glover, John	109
Gray, Sarah	100
Edward	201
Garnsey, Isaac	50
Grant, Thankful	152
Gere, Edward	158
Graves, Joel	189
Abigal	63
Elisha	64
Catherine	64
Edward	64
Edward B.	95
Timothy	96
Goodwin, Rev. D. E.	158
Dea. John	208
Gunn, John	144
Gould, Rev. Vinson	166
Granger, Almira	96
Gilbert, Elizabeth	198
Hills, Jonathan Esq.	207
Holyoke, Mary	108
Hale, Octavia	161
Sarah	120
Almira	120
Rev. Enoch	161
Hayden, Josiah	157
Josiah	158
Hobart, Priscilla	202
Hastings, Hon. John	174
Hunt, Capt. Jared	160
Hayes, Rev. Joel	176
Hinsdale, Rebeckah	189
Huntington, H. B. H.	104
H. S.	104
H. M. H.	104
Huggins, John	119
Hitchcock, Luke	119
Azubah	198
Hosmer, Thomas	13
H. C.	14
H. T.	14
Hunt, Deacon Jonathan	15
John	16
Jonathan	32
Thankful	32
Elizabeth	37
Dea. Ebenezer	37
Col'n Seth	49
John	49
Esther	49
Sarah	66
Hon. Ebenezer	66
Abner	66

INDEX.

	Page.		Page.
Hunt, Sarah	67	Hale, Hezekiah	143
Wm. King	67	Holbrook, Pelatiah	21
Elisabeth	67	Hulbert, James	52
Martha H.	71	Mary	52
Ebenezer	71	Hall, Jonathan	50
Maria L.	71	Healy, Cap. Joshua	180
John	71	Hinsdale, Mehuman	182
Samuel H.	71	Hawks, Col. John	183
David	71	Elizabeth	183
Wealthy	71	Hunt, Hon. Jonathan	194
Luther	76	Susannah	194
Luther	76	Gen. Ardad	195
Medad	76	Sally	195
Susan	76	Arad	195
Frederick	77	Hinsdale,, Rebeckah	109
Ann M.	128	Ingols, Abigal	84
Susan A.	128	Ives, Maj. Mathew	151
Henshaw, Hon. Samuel	72	Ingersol, Paul	151
Eliza	72	Capt. John	152
Martha	72	I. S.	53
Hooker, Lucy A.	120	Judd, Simeon	16
Rev. John	20	Thomas	18
Sarah	43	William	25
John	119	Sylvester	159
Sarah	119	Hannah	160
Richard	120	Solomon	162
Clarissa	120	Hophni	162
Charles	86	Rev. Jonathan	166
Mary	86	Jakubowski, A. A. J. M.	100
Sarah D.	86	Judd, Sylvester	166
Hinckley, Dorothy	78	Jonathan	167
Hon. Samuel	79	David	89
Dolly A.	79	Sarah	89
Dolly A.	79	David	89
Phebe E.	79	Spencer	89
George	79	Eliza S.	89
Hopkins, Maria	70	Charles S.	89
Wille	70	Jack, John	200
Rev. Samuel	135	Keep, Elizabeth	144
Hannum Joseph	69	D. J. Esq	209
Eliza A.	69	Jones, William Esq	209
Hawley, Lidia	24	Hannah	210
Lieut. Joseph	24	Kellogg, Mary	133
Hon. Joseph	24	Anne	154
Rebeka	24	Jonathan	171
Hale, Experience	143	Mary	171

INDEX.

	Page.		Page
Kellogg, Lois	171	Lyman, Elisha	44
Chester	171	Jonathan H.	65
Ira	171	Abigal	77
Kingsbury, Doct. Sam'l.	124	Henry	78
Jemima	124	Thomas	80
Charles L.	124	Parces	80
K. I.	14	Rev. Henry	83
K. B.	17	Jonathan	121
King, Benjamin	15	Submit	155
Hannah	22	Capt'n Azariah	162
Hannah	45	Benjamin	166
Samuel	45	Mary	166
Thankful	42	Mindwell	87
Daniel	42	Joseph	90
Mary	42	Elizabeth	90
John	77	Frances	90
Rachel	77	Gen. William	104
Phineas	165	Jerusha	105
Kingsley, John	32	Ludden, Nathaniel	105
Sarah	33	Lord, Fidelia	159
Suply	33	Lord, Rev. Henry	159
Moses	37	Lord, Rev. Chester	158
Mary	37	Loomis, Amos	17
Mary	45	Lewis, Thankful	49
Enos	83	Lankton, John	61
Rebecca	83	Leonard, Cynthia	137
John	165	Tamer	137
Charles P.	95	Mary	137
Charles B.	95	Harriet	146
Lathrop, Cap. Thomas	185	Delia	146
Le Baron, Doc. Lazarus	202	Langford, Rachel	87
Lothrop, Col. Isaac	203	L. B.	87
Liman, Livt. John	14	L. D.	88
Joseph	14	Mills, Hon. E. H.	80
Moses	15	Sarah	80
Eunice	20	George F.	80
L. M.	20	Miller, Livt. John	18
Lyman, Martha	28	Hannah	19
Catherin	28	Abraham	21
Zadok	29	Mann, Elias	57
Gideon Esq	29	Asenath	58
Abigal	44	Mather, Doc. Saml.	30
Joseph	44	Martha	31
Jemima	48	Mather, William	47
Capt. William	50	Eunice	47
Sophia H.	64	Elisha	48

INDEX.

Name	Page	Name	Page
Mallefuild, John	116	Parsons, Lieut.	23
Mamamach, Joseph	57	Capt. Ebenezer	25
Mason, Capt. David	115	Moses	25
Morris, Caroline	129	Mercy	26
Henry O.	129	Eunice	26
Mix, Rev. Joseph	151	Mary	26
Marsh, Sarah	133	Mary	28
Mills, Benjamin	178	Hannah	32
Mary	179	Lieut. John	33
Morgan, Lieut. Nathan	140	Lieut. William	50
Miller, Thomas	141	Mary	49
Abigal	141	Mary	62
Mirrick, Dea. Joseph	141	Phineas	63
Mary	142	Phineas Jun.	63
Sarah	142	Nancy	63
Lieut. James	142	John	159
Francis	179	Lydia	160
Mosely, Capt. John	153	Elizabeth	164
Montague, Peter	162	Rev. David	168
Matson, Maria E.	99	Eunice	168
Moies, John	94	Moses	96
Anna	94	Pease, Richard S.	92
Elizabeth R.	94	Pvmry, Dea. Medad	16
McNiel, Hannah	197	Pomeroy, Capt. John	33
Moore, Rev. Z. S.	172	Col. Seth	34
Merrill, Capt. Calvin	170	Mary	37
Mattoon, Gen. Ebenezer	170	Lydia	44
Montague, Lieut. Luke	176	Dea. Ebenezer	48
Merriam, Capt. Joseph	207	Phœbe	52
Eunice	207	Rachel	53
North, Nancy	63	Elizabeth	50
Hannah A.	63	Quartus	51
Noble, Abigal	149	Sarah	66
Nash, Thomas	157	Asahel	75
Newton, Sebra	189	Hannah	75
Rev. Roger	189	Susannah	75
Newcomb, Mary	189	Miriam	75
Osgood, Henry	120	Lucretia	75
Mary S.	120	Judith	76
Parsons,	15	Lemuel	165
Wait	15	Capt. Elisha	88
Sarah	21	Price, Dea. Benjamin	179
Capt. John	21	Perkins, Rev. Nathan	169
Joseph Esq.	24	Porter, Capt. Moses	132
John	25	Elizabeth	134
Elizabeth	25	Eleazer	135

INDEX. 219

	Page.
Partridge, Oliver	175
Anna	175
Park, Gen. Wareham	153
Phœnix, Elizabeth	69
Phelps, Abigal	20
Mary	27
Samuel	27
Pynchon, Edward	113
Willi'm	113
Hon. John	111
Amy	111
William	111
Mahitable	112
Hon. John	112
Margaret	112
John	112
Bathshua	112
Phebe	112
John	112
William	112
Katherine	112
Hon. Joseph	112
Edward	112
William	113
Sarah	113
George	113
Maj. William	113
Lucy	113
John	113
Prescott, Ebenezer	29
Preston, John	175
Packard, J. H.	120
Pitkin, William Esq.	206
Russell, Stephen	119
Archelaus	119
Rebekah	131
Rev. John	132
R. M.	86
Russell, Rachel	89
Laura	90
Rumrill, Susan	142
Root, John	149
Moses	151
Dea. Joseph	152
Robbins, Jane	199
Sellon, Dr. William F.	171
Seymour, Sarah N.	192

	Page
St. * * * Noah	18
Strong, Eben	22
Eben	22
Aaron	22
Ensign Noah	45
Jonathan	47
Elizabeth	47
Caleb	48
Phebe	48
Rev. Joseph	158
Jane	158
Jonathan	87
Rachel	87
Caleb	97
Sarah	97
Sarah	97
Edward	97
Phebe	98
Philip	98
Julia A.	98
Elizabeth C.	98
Julia M.	98
Rev. Caleb	98
Maria C.	99
Theodore	99
Julia A.	99
Martha A.	99
Sarah H.	99
Simeon	171
Shepherd Thomas	94
Catherine	94
Elizabeth	94
Smith, Col. William	113
James B	129
Ensigne Chileab	131
Rev. Jonathan	134
Chester	134
Experience	96
Smih, Ilizabeth	133
Stockbridge, Elizabeth	129
Dorothy A.	129
Scott, John	167
Sargeant, Thomas	126
Jr.	126
Ellen	127
Mary	127
Snow, Cordelia	90

INDEX.

	Page.		Page.
Smeed, Mindwell	42	Turner, David	57
Starkweather, Charles	62	Electa	57
Roxana	62	Achsa	51
Patty	62	Sofia	51
Sikes, Mary	116	Thayer, Sarah	159
Ensign Increase	116	Asa	161
Mary	116	Tappan, Benjamin	68
Stearns, William A.	129	George	68
Sanborn, Susan	121	Sarah	68
Scutt, Capt James	126	Taylor, Margaret	143
Elizabeth	126	Samuel	150
Sheldon, Katron	16	Rev. Edward	150
Dea Thomas	25	Rhoda	150
Mary	35	Hon. Eldad	150
Ebenezer	35	Thankful	150
Stokes, Rev. R. S.	145	Ruth	151
Sheldon, Noah	150	Capt. James	154
Stoddard, Rev. Sol.	23	Benjamin	180
Esther	31	Tabor, Charlotte S.	100
Hon. John	34	Tute, Jonathan	191
Prudence	34	Amos	194
Hannah	34	Jemima	194
Martha	42	James	194
Eunice	43	Townsend, Robert	210
David	43	Upham,	87
Solomon Esq.	43	Watson, George	203
Esther	43	Wright, Mary	17
Arthur F.	84	Samuel	23
William B.	84	Sarah	23
David T.	84	Hezekiah	30
Solomon	100	John	31
Stebbins, Gideon	26	Anne	32
Rowland	54	Phebe	33
Thomas	54	Experience	39
Joseph	54	Capt. Noah	39
Joseph	54	Sarah	39
Joseph	54	Miriam	39
Mary	54	Selah	46
Joseph	54	Esther	46
Eunice	54	Asa	55
Clarissa	53	Noah	52
Festus	130	Timothy	51
Sherman, Roger	209	Elizabeth	51
Tillotson, Hervey	83	Elizabeth M. C.	72
Todd, William	62	Asahel	72
Thompson, Mary C.	108	Asahel	72

INDEX. 221

	Page.		Page
Wright Henry,	72	Walker, Jacob	174
Harriet	72	Whipple, Timothy	198
Elizabeth	73	White, Job	73
Ephraim	78	Lewis	73
Moses	78	Eunice	138
Lieut. Abel	110	Persis	179
Benjamin	116	Mary	180
Catherine	163	Wells, Abigal	35
Capt. Stephen	163	Sarah H.	89
Esther	164	Dea. Thomas	184
Hezekiah	102	Obed	186
Theodore	103	Williams, Rev. Sol.	68
Seth	103	Miranda	58
Georgiana	103	Julia	59
Woodbridge, Rev. Timothy	174	Mrs. Mary	58
John	176	Eleazer	128
Col. Ruggles	176	Charlotte	128
Tryphena	176	Hon. Israel	173
Martha	176	Sarah	174
Warriner, Enos James	125	Col Ephraim	182
Martha	125	Thomas	182
Lieut. James	125	Rev. John	183
Thomas	125	Eunice	183
Ensn Ebenezer	125	Abigal	183
Whitfield, Rev. George	199	Webster, John	135
Worner, Eleazer	133	Worthington, Mary	146
Ware, Wm. H.	124	Seth	146
Mary E.	124	Capt. Jona.	147
Westgarre, John	131	Phœbe	147
Waldo, Clarissa	104	Sybil	147
Warnen, Mary	173	Lucy	148
Warner, Titus	172	Job	148
Sarah	179	John	148
Daniel	64	Abia	148
Phœbe	64	Wells, Asa	189
Whitney, Sarah W.	91	Williams, Jerymy R.	207
William D.	91	Wood, Obadiah	205
Margaretta	92	Williams, Rev. Eliph. D. D.	205
Alice C.	92	Woodbridge, Content	206
Ellen D.	92	Williams, Mary	208
Mercy	198	Wolcott, Roger Esq.	208
Washburn, Rev. Royal	168	Wright, Sarah	103
Whitman, Elizabeth	204	Sarah	105
Wait, Ebenezer	19	Samuel	105
Simeon	165	Yeomans, James	154
Wood, David G.	87		

19*

ERRATA, OMISSIONS, &C.

J. Lyman, p. 135, died and was buried at York, Me.

In annals, p. xi. Rev. E. P. Rogers, now of Augusta, Ga., was pastor of the Edwards Church, from 1844, to 1848.

Methodist Church organized 1843; Rev. W. Ward, first pastor, succeeded by M. Dwight, W. R. Bagnell, C. Baker, and J. W. Mowry.

P. xii. The pastors of the Baptist Church have been Rev. B. Willard, Abel Brown, Wm. M. Doolittle, H. D. Doolittle, D. M. Crane.

1850. Leeds post-office established, Tho. Musgrave, post-master.

Page 8, for 500, Church, &c. read 100.

Page 57, read his for her, 17th line.

Page 192, 3d line, for employed, read improved.

Page 192, 18th line for, of this town, read of Hinsdale, N. H.

Page 57, Mr Josiah Clark, Ætat 92.

Page 59. In the 54th year of his age, under 4th line of Joseph Cook's Epitaph.

Page 62, for June 33, read June 23.

THE ancestor of the families of DAY, found in Springfield, West Springfield, South Hadley, and Northampton, was ROBERT DAY, one of the first settlers of Hartford, Conn. who emigrated from England to this country in 1634, and died in 1648, aged 44. His eldest son, THOMAS, settled at Springfield, and died Dec. 27, 1711. Most of the families of the name in Springfield, and West Springfield are descended from him. His other son, JOHN, from whom are descended the families in South Hadley, and Northampton, (with one or two exceptions,) lived in Hartford, and died in that place about 1730. A genealogical register of the numerous descendants of ROBERT DAY, among whom is Rev. JEREMIAH DAY, D. D., late President of Yale College, containing more than two thousand five hundred names, was published at Northampton in 1848, in an octavo pamphlet 130 pages.

N. B. Many inscriptions are in the hands of the compiler, which could not be inserted in this book, but which are reserved for another edition or another volume.

PATRONS OF THIS PUBLICATION.

AMHERST.
Edward Dickinson 5
Aaron Warner
A. M. Colton
J. S. & C. Adams
J. R. Cushman
Job Cushman

BOSTON.
Wm. B. Calhoun
Charles H. Mills 5
Samuel Henshaw 5
Isaac C. Bates 5
John Tappan 2
Charles Tappan
Joseph Hawley Dorr
D. P. King 4
J. P. Jewett
Charles Stoddard
Holman & Silsby
Joseph B. Felt
J. Henshaw
Albert Fearing
J. H. Wright
Theodore M. Smith 3
J. W. Clark
Levi Ingols
Charles Mayo
A. L. Strong
William Dwight
E. M. Wright 5
George Dickinson
Charles A. Mann

Isaac Newton
Andrew H. Ward
J. W. Wright
James Savage 2
Charles Ewer
Samuel G. Drake
J. Wingate Thornton

CAMBRIDGE.
Edward Everett
J. E. Worcester
Jared Sparks
Charles Beck 5
H. W. Longfellow 3
Theophilus Parsons
Dan'l Treadwell
Charles Lowell

MEDFORD.
A. B. Warner

GREENFIELD.
Geo. T. Davis 3
W. T. Davis
H. W. Clapp
H. Chapman
Titus Strong
John Russell
L. L. Graves
E. P. Graves
A. F. Stone 2
Ansel Phelps
L. Merriam
Edwin A. Clark
Edward Dewey

PATRONS OF THIS PUBLICATION.

SPRINGFIELD.
George Ashmun 3
Ffed Dwight 5
Edward A. Morris 2
David K. Lee 2
John B. Stebbins 2
R. A. Chapman 2
Cyrus Cole 2
Richard Bliss 2
James D. Brewer
James Brewer 2d
Henry Brewer Jr.
Samuel L. Parsons
Geo. W. Rice
Charles Stearns
S. D. Holman
S. Upson
Samuel Bowles
J. G. Holland
Joel Kendall
Rufus Sikes
R. Shurtleff
Edward W. Gere
W. W. Lee
Lewis Warriner
G. & C. Merriam
A. G. Pease
Josiah Hooker
John Hooker
E. W. Dickinson
C. P. Nichols
Simon Sanborn
Elam Stockbridge
Josiah B. Allen
E. A. Holcomb
William Bridgman
Lucius C. Allin
Joseph H. Damon

Isaac Rindge Jr.
L. H. Gaylord
A. C. Markham
C. White
O. A. Seamans
Geo. W. Mirick
Luke Bardwell
L. F. Kellogg
W. W. Kellogg
Robt. Crossett
Lorenzo Norton
William Bryant
Henry Smith

WORCESTER.
Francis H. Dewey

EASTHAMPTON.
J. P. Snow

HADLEY.
John Woodbridge
Joseph Smith
Elihu Dickinson
Eleazer Porter
Samuel S. Hibbard

HATFIELD.
Josiah Brown

WEST SPRINGFIELD.
Sewall White
Daniel Merrick

SOUTH HADLEY.
David Turner
Alonzo Bardwell

LONGMEADOW.
Geo. W. Callender

HAYDENVILLE.
Joe Hayden 10

NORTHAMPTON.
Daniel Stebbins 4
Benjamin Barrett 2
William Allen 3

PATRONS OF THIS PUBLICATION.

J. H. Butler 4
John G. Musgrave 2
Henry Bright 2
Miles G. Moies 5
John Hannum 2
Cephas Clark 2
Charles A. Dewey 5
Benjamin North 2
Martin B Graves 2
Daniel W. Clark 2
J. Boies
George E. Day
James Hibben
Lewis Strong
J. D. Whitney
S. L. Hinckley
Osmyn Baker
Eliph. Williams
Daniel Thompson 2
Ansel Wright 2
James Thompson
Sylvester Bridgman
John Bridgman
Sidney E. Bridgman
Joseph C. Bridgman
Edward Warner
W. A. Arnold
W. F. Arnold
William Pease
Cordial Crane
A. W. Thayer
Lewis S. Hopkins
S. W. Hopkins
Ebenezer Phelps
William C. Prentiss
George Cook
C. M. Kinney
Elijah Abbott

Edwin Kingsley
Lyman Kingsley
Quartus Kingsley
N. H. Felton
Samuel Wells
J. D. Wells
Eliel Barnard
Asahel S. Abell
A. G. Abell
M. T. Moody
Joseph S. Brown
Charles C. Clapp
Levi Strong
Enos Clark
John Lyman Clark
Amasa D. Wade
J. H. Fowle
J. P. Strong
T. J. Trundy
Chauncey Clark
Sylvester Graham
David Strong
Seth Hunt
Josiah Hunt
Joel Hunt
Henry S. Gere
S. M. Smith
Charles F. Graves
Thomas Pomeroy
Edward Parsons
S. C. Parsons
Lyman Parsons
Josiah Parsons
Edward C. Strong
Josiah W. Smith
William H. Stoddard
Solomon Stoddard
C. K. Hawks

PATRONS OF THIS PUBLICATION.

Charles Collins
T. B. Hutchins
L. L. Simonds
Ebenezer Hancock
William B. Atkins
J. & L. Metcalf
Daniel Kingsley
H. K. Starkweather, jr.
Edward Clarke
Hervey Smith
J. R. Dickinson
Moses D. Clark
J. S. Lathrop
Horace Lyman
Isaac Damon, jr.
Theodore Sheldon
Jacob Parsons
Alpheus Lyman
Joseph B. Lyman
James Clapp
Porter Underwood
Isaac Damon
A. P. Peck
Rufus Ellis
D. M. Crane
Jabez French
Charles Walker
Theodore Burt
John B. Graves
James Dunlap
Christopher Clarke
Pliny Russell
George Burrows
Justin Cook
William Lawrence
Isaac Clark
A. H. Edwards
Oliver Judd

David Joy
Porter Nutting
Ansel Jewett
Thomas Walsh
William F. Pratt
Samuel R. Baxter
Hiram Stebbins
William A. Hawley
Joseph Allen

WESTHAMPTON.

Joel Cook
Julius Cook
Enoch H. Clark } *Philad'a*
E. H. Butler
T. M. Hunt, *Auburn, N. Y.*
H. Lathrop, *Savannah, Ga.*
L. T. Stoddard, *Boston.*
A. T. Stoddard, *Glas'w Sct'd.*
William Choice, *Greenville, S. C*, 10
David C. Judd, *Spartanburgh, S. C*, 3
Silas Binney, *Weymouth*
Erastus Rodman } *Williams-*
Fred'ck Thayer } *burgh*
J. C. Clark, *Jenksville.*
Myron Lawrence } *Belcher-*
Porter Bridgman } *town.*
Park Warner, *Granby*
Thomas Robbins, *Hartford, Conn.*, 2
J. B. Bridgman, *Sacramento, California.*
William Ames, *Dedham*, 2.

BRATTLEBORO, VT.

W. H. Rockwell
R. Wesselhœf
John B. Miner

PATRONS OF THIS PUBLICATION.

George H. Salisbury
J. W. Campbell
Roswell Hunt 2
J. J. Crandall
Albert Worthington
Geo. W. Pratt
Jean Bisonette
E. J. Carpenter
George Howe
Morris Butler 4 *Buffalo, N. Y.*

John Hunt } *Vernon, Vt.*
E. Howe

E. H. Barston } *Walpole,*
W. P. Tilden } *N. H.*

NEW YORK.

George M. Snow
Henry Edwards 2
Sumner Clark